DEVOTIONAL VENTURES

COREY CLEEK
GENERAL EDITOR

Regal

From Gospel Light
Ventura, California, U.S.A.

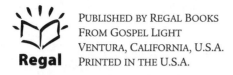

PUBLISHED BY REGAL BOOKS
FROM GOSPEL LIGHT
VENTURA, CALIFORNIA, U.S.A.
Regal PRINTED IN THE U.S.A.

Regal Books is a ministry of Gospel Light, a Christian publisher dedicated to serving the local church. We believe God's vision for Gospel Light is to provide church leaders with biblical, user-friendly materials that will help them evangelize, disciple and minister to children, youth and families.

It is our prayer that this Regal book will help you discover biblical truth for your own life and help you meet the needs of others. May God richly bless you.

For a free catalog of resources from Regal Books/Gospel Light, please call your Christian supplier or contact us at 1-800-4-GOSPEL *or* www.regalbooks.com.

Library of Congress Cataloging-in-Publication Data
Devotional ventures / edited by Corey Cleek.
  p. cm.
 ISBN 0-8307-4314-6 (hard cover)
  1. Employees—Religious life. 2. Employees—Prayer-books and devotions—English. 3. Work—Prayer-books and devotions—English. 4. Work—Religious aspects—Christianity. 5. Devotional exercises. I. Cleek, Corey.
  BV4593.D48 2006
  242'.68—dc22   2006027549

1   2   3   4   5   6   7   8   9   10   /   10   09   08   07

Rights for publishing this book in other languages are contracted by Gospel Light Worldwide, the international nonprofit ministry of Gospel Light. Gospel Light Worldwide also provides publishing and technical assistance to international publishers dedicated to producing Sunday School and Vacation Bible School curricula and books in the languages of the world. For additional information, visit www.gospellightworldwide.org; write to Gospel Light Worldwide, P.O. Box 3875, Ventura, CA 93006; or send an e-mail to info@gospellightworldwide.org.

CONTENTS

ACKNOWLEDGMENTS

There are many ongoing contributors to the Devotional Ventures project, both those who contribute writings for publication and those who work behind the scenes to make this project possible.

Thank you . . .

To the Devotional Ventures partner ministries for your commitment to this project and for your ongoing outreach, discipleship and training for business professionals around the world, including:

- Priority Associates—Craig Seibert and Timothy McCoach
- Intervarsity—John Terrill
- equip—Brett Johnson and Kim Daus-Edwards

To Nebo Group, and in particular to Ryan MacCarthy, for your commitment to the creation and ongoing development of the Devotional Ventures website.

To Regal Books: Alex, Marlene, Roger and to the extended Regal Books and Gospel Light team, for your commitment to providing an opportunity through this project for business people to explore the intersection of faith and business.

To Paul Barger, Matt Mathias and Kim Daus-Edwards, for investing the time to review the writing submissions and provide valuable input and feedback.

To Jeff Rogers, Nancy Ortberg, John Brandon, Wally Hawley, Katherine Leary, Duane Moyer, Bill Leonard, Dave Dias and Brad Lomenick, for your mentorship, introductions and encouragement.

To the Devotional Ventures contributing writers, for your transparency and willingness to share your experiences, passions and reflections with us.

And to our Lord and Savior Jesus Christ, for Your love, forgiveness, guidance and the blessing of having the opportunity to worship and serve You while expressing our passions as business professionals.

Thank you.

FOREWORD

I became a Christian shortly after starting work at Intel. As with any new job, I wanted to do well, and thus I was especially motivated to succeed at my new company. I immersed myself in my new field, company and career and was anxious to work long hours, not because I needed to, but because I loved my job and didn't want to stop!

I had come from a farming background and was used to working long hours. Working inside Intel was great. It was air conditioned, clean and safe. Compared to enduring a hot, humid day on the farm, working in hay and dirt and having to be careful not to get kicked by a horse or bull, Intel was a paradise. I was getting paid more than I earned on the farm—even getting paid extra for overtime. Now that was a first! I was loving my job and pouring myself 101 percent into it.

In addition to my long hours at Intel, I was also going to school almost full time to complete my bachelors degree in electrical engineering. School in the morning, work in the afternoon, and study and work at night. Life was hectic, but I loved every second of it. I was consuming everything I could about computers and semiconductors and felt that

I had found the perfect career path.

However, after becoming a Christian, I felt this enormous spiritual burden to go into ministry. Day and night I anguished over the thought of leaving the career path that seemed to be unfolding so perfectly in front of me. As everything was falling into place and I was doing extremely well in school and work, I couldn't imagine that God was so quickly calling me to a different path. After months of prayer and thought on the question, I was no closer to a resolution, and I was still terribly conflicted as to what God was doing in my life. Finally, I decided to lay this situation before God

When I did so, for the first time I had almost immediate peace about the situation. Slowly, God began to reveal to me that my workplace *was* my ministry. A few of us are called to vocational ministry, and in that role we apply our full-time energies as ministers for Christ. The rest of us are called as full-time ministers but do it in the context and setting of our full-time employment. I'm a full-time minister for Jesus Christ, and Intel is paying my salary. I'm a workplace minister. I'm a marketplace missionary.

This devotional was written by workplace ministers for workplace ministers. It was written by people struggling to live out their faith each day and be obedient to God's call. The authors are people just like you who've been living out their faith during the days, weeks and years of their jobs and careers. Each one of them has had failures and successes along the journey. We pray you find this book useful and encouraging in your journey each day.

Pat Gelsinger
Senior Vice President
General Manager, Digital Enterprise Group
Intel Corporation

Introduction

Have you ever wondered what Jesus would be like as a vice president of marketing? A financial analyst? A sales manager? A venture capitalist? A CEO? How would He manage His time? How would He make decisions? How would He lead and manage teams? How would He manage money? How would He balance the devotion to His work and the devotion to His family and community?

As we seek to emulate Jesus in the marketplace and beyond, it is important for us to remember that we are not alone. There are business people of all ages, professions, genders and races living in cities across the globe who are seeking to live the way Jesus would live His life today as a business professional.

Devotional Ventures is a representation of the passions, surprises, challenges, praises and reflections of the multitude of business people around the world who are seeking to live lives devoted to Jesus. We welcome you to join us in the journey.

GLORIFYING GOD WHEN ON HOLD

BRETT JOHNSON

PRESIDENT, THE INSTITUTE FOR INNOVATION,
INTEGRATION AND IMPACT

May those who delight in my vindication shout for joy and gladness.

PSALM 35:27

"Lord," said Martha to Jesus, "if you had been here, my brother would not have died" (John 11:21). She and her sister, Martha, had sent word two days before to Jesus that their brother, Lazarus, was ill. But Jesus had tarried where He was, and now it seemed too late—their brother had died.

Sometimes, we all feel like Mary and Martha, desperate for Jesus to show up exactly when we need Him to show up. Yet when God delays in answering our prayers (such as the healing of Lazarus—it didn't happen!), it is for the purpose of His answering in a different way (such as raising Lazarus from the dead). God does this so that He will receive more glory and so that we will know He is God. As Jesus said to His disciples:

> This sickness will not end in death. No, it is for God's glory so that God's Son may be glorified through it (John 11:4).

When God delays in prospering our businesses or promoting our newest product, it is so that we may die to our own ideas, our own egos. After the delay, we often experience the joy of experiencing God's best for us.

As the psalmist states, "May those who delight in my vindication shout for joy and gladness." When God vindicates His servant leaders, He does so that we may shout for joy and gladness and say, "The Lord be exalted, who delights in the well-being of His servant" (Psalm 35:27).

In my career and business, I seek to find this vision that will enable me to press through the difficulties and sacrifices that come with pursuing His purpose. The one common theme that has the capacity to cause me to pull together in harmony and without self-destruction is the glory of God. The long delay, the death of self, the growing desire for God's fame, the eventual vindication . . . I will experience them all as the theory and practice of doing business with God converge.

POINT TO PONDER

GOD SOMETIMES PUTS US ON HOLD SO THAT, AFTER THE WAIT,
THERE IS LESS OF US AND MORE OF HIM.

QUESTIONS TO CONSIDER

1. Does your knowledge and enjoyment of God raise the bar until people see beyond you to the ultimate goal of glorifying God?

2. Like Martha, do you ever get so frustrated by a situation that you miss God's greater purpose? How would keeping your eyes and heart focused on God change your perspective when life goes crazy?

3. What do you need to do once you recognize God's sovereign will and power in your life?

MISSIONARY ECONOMIST

RANDY RAGGIO

MARKETING PROFESSOR, LOUISIANA STATE UNIVERSITY

2

What is more, I consider everything a loss compared to the surpassing greatness of knowing Christ Jesus my Lord, for whose sake I have lost all things. I consider them rubbish, that I may gain Christ.

PHILIPPIANS 3:7

If you have ever wondered if the economic principles that govern business practices are compatible with the biblical principles that govern our personal practices, consider the fact that Paul uses an opportunity-cost argument in Philippians 3:7-8.

In economics, an opportunity cost is the value of an opportunity passed up, or foregone. For example, if your job pays $30 per hour but you could get a job that would pay $45 per hour for the same effort (and all other things being equal), then you are giving up (it is costing you) $15 per hour to work for your current employer. That $15 per hour is your opportunity cost.

If we define an economy as "a system that sets values for the utilization of resources," then it is obvious that Paul must be talking about another economy entirely, one that assigns different values to both resources and rewards—same stuff, different values.

Consider the words "profit," "loss," "rubbish" and "gain" in Philippians 3:7-8. Paul was saying that there were many things in his life that were profitable—they returned more than they cost in human economy terms—but compared with the alternative, "the surpassing greatness of knowing Christ Jesus," the profit came up short. Both returns are on the positive side of the ledger, but in God's economy, there is a greater return for the same effort.

I am in the middle of a job search and am fortunate to have a choice between two good options. One option means more money, prestige and opportunities for more of both in the future, which I could certainly use to advance the cause of Christ, but it also means a more single-minded focus on my career for the next few years. The other option would still surpass my material needs but may produce a greater gain according to God's value. Faced with a decision between two profitable options, it is a comfort to know that the Bible has advice for my economic decisions. As I consider Paul's lesson in economics, I pray that God will reveal His greater value to me.

James 2:17 says that all good gifts come from God, even our jobs and the rewards it brings. Recognize the source of those gifts and seek to know what He would have you do with them. Remember that there's an opportunity cost to pursuing the things of this world. God has a different economy. Hear it in the Sermon on the Mount. Read it in Paul's letters. See it in Christ's life. And experience it in your own.

POINT TO PONDER

RECOGNIZE GOD'S ECONOMIC MEASUREMENT OF
YOUR JOB AND THE REWARDS IT BRINGS.

QUESTIONS TO CONSIDER

1. When you think of your own life, where are you investing in the wrong economy?

2. In God's economy, what things are you doing that will reap rewards in heaven? What specific things could you do better or differently to focus on God's eternal economy?

3. Have you experienced God's economy already in your life? In what ways have you seen God's economy at work?

Is God Real to You?

Tom Tison

PRESIDENT, TISON AND SHELTON CONSULTING

3

> *Trust in the LORD with all your heart and lean not on your*
> *own understanding; in all your ways acknowledge him,*
> *and he will make your paths straight.*
>
> PROVERBS 3:5-6

I absolutely cherish the above passage in Proverbs. It first became real to me during the summer before my junior year in college. I had committed to do something totally outside my comfort zone—to move to a new state and sell Bibles and educational books door to door. At the time, I was definitely not a salesperson.

That summer in south Georgia proved to be life changing. Not only did I start learning the value of good communication skills, how a positive attitude could positively affect everything around me, and how without hard work success will not happen, but I also learned to rely on Jesus Christ.

I grew up in a good Christian home and even attended Christian schools, but I never truly relied on Jesus. I never had to. Except for the occasional "Lord, please help me on this test" or "Please help our team win," most of my wants and desires were accomplished by myself or by my parents. I share this with you so that you can examine your life and see if you have ever truly relied on Him.

For me, I never earnestly asked God to direct my paths until that summer when I was selling books. For the first time in my life, I was away from everything I knew and was doing something I had never done before. I needed help.

It's interesting how in times of need, people tend to fall back on the truths taught to them by those who love them. I thank God for the Christian home in which I was raised that provided me with a firm foundation. I started to read the Bible in a different way. I read and wanted God to speak to me through His Word. With sweat and tears, I prayed to God Almighty for guidance. I told Him my wants and desires, even though He already knew them. That summer, God became real to me.

Is God real to you?

Do you read His Word and ask for guidance? My experience tells me that unless you are doing something tough and unfamiliar, your Christian acts of reading the Bible and praying can turn into just that—an act.

So I encourage you to do something out of your comfort zone, and then get ready to grow. Even though the unknown can be scary, take hold of Proverbs 3:5-6:

> Trust in the LORD with all your heart and lean not on your own understanding; in all your ways acknowledge Him, and He will make your paths straight.

POINT TO PONDER

DON'T BE AFRAID OF THE UNCERTAIN.
GOD WILL GUIDE YOU.

QUESTIONS TO CONSIDER

1. Are you feeling uncertain or worried about anything today? As you think about the areas of your life in which you have been feeling unsure, read Proverbs 3:5-6 again and ask God to show you His guidance.

2. Have you recently seen God's guidance in your life?

3. Are you letting God guide you in your life situations today? Are there areas in your life over which you have tight control but need to release to God?

CAN YOU DEFEND CHRISTIANITY?

REGI CAMPBELL

PRINCIPAL, SEEDSOWER INVESTMENTS

4

A new command I give you: Love one another. As I have
loved you, so you must love one another.

JOHN 13:34

In *Blue Like Jazz*, Donald Miller shocked me when he described an interview he did with a radio talk show host.

"Defend Christianity," demanded the radio jock.

"I can't," replied Miller.

In disbelief, the host asked again, "What do you mean? You write Christian books and stuff. You can't even defend what you write about?"

Miller explained that today, Christianity means too many different things to people. To some, it's the guy holding up the "John 3:16" sign in the end zone of the football field. To others, it's the obnoxious pink-haired lady on TBN, crying and begging for your money. All around, people who wear the brand name "Christian" often repulse those who aren't believers . . . rarely do they compel them.

When I first committed myself to Christ in 1983, I was dangerous. I wanted to save everybody. I telephoned every adult in my family to confront them about their faith. I a-mused friends with my insensitive zeal. And the net result of all my talking? Zero new Christians.

Several people, including my own brother and sister, saw me as self-righteous and judgmental . . . two words that were never used to describe Jesus. As a matter of fact, the only two adjectives Jesus ever used to describe Himself were "gentle" and "humble in heart."

The "secret sauce" of Christianity is Jesus. Yes, Jesus! Even the name is just plain hard to process. Yet we need to recognize that Jesus has no other physical presence on this earth except through people like us. We are His hands, His feet, His eyes, His handshake. If Jesus is going to communicate His love and acceptance to people, it's going to be through us.

Now don't get me wrong; there's a time to be bold about your faith and even confrontational with the people that you've earned the right to do this with. But we do have to earn that right and they have to know that we care before they will care to know.

So today, we have the opportunity to communicate the love and acceptance of Jesus Christ to every human being we encounter. We have the ability to share the love of Christ with our bosses, our coworkers, our friends, our families and even to the strangers we meet on the street.

We have the privilege of being His light in a dark world:

> You are the light of the world. A city on a hill cannot be hidden. Neither do people light a lamp and put it under a bowl. . . . In the same way, let your light shine before men, that they may see your good deeds and praise your Father in heaven (Matthew 5:14-16).

So, will we do it? Will we intentionally let Jesus express His delight in people—whom He created in His own image? Will we set aside our judgmental self-righteousness and look at others the way Jesus does? Can we leave the judging of people to God and just love people as Jesus does . . . one encounter at a time?

POINT TO PONDER

AS THE BODY OF CHRIST, WE ARE JESUS PERSONIFIED.

QUESTIONS TO CONSIDER

1. Do you ever find yourself judging others at work? Do you find yourself comparing yourself to others? Does it make you feel any better? How does Jesus see these people? Will you choose to see them as He does?

2. How will you defend Christianity to those you work with? Will you be a witness through your actions and by genuinely loving and serving others?

3. What do you think it means to say that "we are Jesus personified"? How can you activate this personification in your work life?

INVESTING IN ETERNITY

DOUG SCHWEITZER

PRESIDENT, ADA, INC.

5

Do not store up for yourselves treasures on earth, where moth and rust destroy, and where thieves break in and steal.

MATTHEW 6:19

The world in which we live grants us limitless opportunities to build our own personal wealth and increase our net worth. We have financial goals for each and every area of our lives. We have plans for how to reach a standard of living we desire, plans for retiring in comfort, plans for affording our children's education, and plans for achieving every other thing this world deems important to our life here on Earth.

Being surrounded by successful professionals from all different vocations, we can begin to adopt a way of thinking that is not eternal but temporal. However, Jesus tells us that we should not lay up for ourselves treasures on Earth but in heaven, "for where your treasure is, there your heart will be also" (Matthew 6:21).

Whatever we put our finances into automatically gives us an added interest on that investment. For example, if we invest heavily in company X, we will have an added interest in how well company X performs in the market. Our treasure (money) is there, so our heart will be there also.

I have come to realize that by putting more of my money into missions, I have inherently developed a greater love and vision for missions. More of my treasure is there and, consequently, so is more of my heart.

I have always believed in the importance of missions. However, it was not until I put more of my treasure into missions that I found more of my heart was there as well. When I took this step of faith, two things happened: First, God provided for me, and second, I experienced a new level of relationship with God because of the faith I exercised. Two simple principles have since helped me trust God with more of the finances He brings my way:

Principle 1: Faith. I know that it is impossible to out-give God, and by faith I have committed to let God prove Himself to me.

Principle 2: Belief. I believe that every dollar given for the cause of Christ has an eternal return that is impossible to compete with temporally.

The Maker of the universe has promised to supply our every need according to His riches in glory by Christ Jesus (see Philippians 4:19). James 4:14-15 tells us:

> Why, you do not even know what will happen tomorrow. You are a mist that appears for a little while and then vanishes. Instead, you ought to say, "If it is the Lord's will, we will live and do this or that."

We are not even guaranteed tomorrow, much less reaching retirement. But I should be clear: I believe it is wise and prudent to plan for tomorrow, as long as it is not at the expense of being cheap with God. The bottom line is whether we are investing more in the things of heaven or the things of Earth. Our checkbooks will let us know what is most important to us.

I have never known a greater sense of fulfillment and blessing than when I exercised faith with increased giving and allowed God to prove Himself. Knowing that all I have belongs to God gives me the confidence to support ministries and individuals committed to the cause of Christ.

I set goals every year in many areas of my life, but none is more rewarding than my tithes and offerings goal. It is a goal that is rewarding on Earth, and it will also be one day in heaven.

POINT TO PONDER

ARE YOU EXPERIENCING THE BLESSINGS OF GIVING?

QUESTIONS TO CONSIDER

1. If this life is a mist, how can you invest in eternity by tangibly blessing another person today through giving?

2. Could you feasibly double the amount you give this month?

3. In what areas do you feel led to give more of your resources: international missions? orphans? a tithe to the church? local or regional nonprofit organizations?

DOING BUSINESS IN LIGHT OF COMPASSION

ANDY LIU

CEO, ADVANCED MEDIA RESEARCH GROUP, INC.

6

What good will it be for a man if he gains the whole world, yet forfeits
his soul? Or what can a man give in exchange for his soul?

MATTHEW 16:26

Brennan Manning once said, "We are never more like Christ
than when we are choked with compassion for the brokenness of others." As an entrepreneur who makes decisions
based on return on investment, it sometimes seems as if
I am allowing compassion for others to take a back seat. I've
frequently struggled with how the profit motive melds with
my spiritual conscience and beliefs.

Often, I hear from friends who are serving in Sudan,
Peru, Rwanda and Russia. They are living God's calling to
serve the poor and the marginalized and are making a difference. Am I contributing to the brokenness of others?

Am I so consumed with my profit motive that I lose track of eternity and the calling on my life to have compassion and serve the "least of these"?

In 1 Corinthians 15:58, Paul states, "Always give yourselves fully to the work of the Lord because you know that your labor in the Lord is not in vain." During my last start-up, there were many days in which I felt my labor was in vain because I believed I wasn't doing the work of the Lord. The long hours seemed to keep my focus off center.

I came to realize that my main motive for work was too shortsighted and focused strictly on maximizing profit. This led to some real soul-searching on my part and learning how to base my motivation for work on compassion. I eventually found the answer by going on trips with workers to developing countries. I caught the vision for my life to serve the poor by creating opportunities through business and other economic means in order to build a sustained economic and spiritual base in these nations.

I recently came back from El Salvador absolutely energized about the impact a small group of engineers and business people had on a poor community in Central America. We completed a tech center where people who live on one to two dollars a day can learn critical computer skills that will allow them to seek employment and provide more dignity and sustenance for their families. We're now looking into

35

partnering with the locals to create a for-profit business that will employ the poor who are trained in the tech center.

Leveraging the gifts that God gave me in economic means and in business acumen has been instrumental in giving me a greater perspective on eternity. All the fruits of my labor are His, and I will continue to use them in bettering the lives of others. Knowing this, I am even more motivated to build a *great* company.

Point to Ponder

In the workplace, compassion can be
a powerful motivator.

Questions to Consider

1. When was the last time you showed compassion through your gifts in the workplace? How did it change a situation or your perspective?

2. What kinds of gifts do you have that you can leverage for others?

3. How are you using your gifts to show genuine compassion to the poor and marginalized today?

Living in a Secret Place

Brent Milligan

PROFESSIONAL MUSICIAN AND MUSIC PRODUCER

7

He who dwells in the shelter of the Most High will
rest in the shadow of the Almighty.

PSALM 91:1

Have you ever been in the midst of a really stressful day at
work and suddenly wished you could escape to a quiet, peaceful, life-giving place?

The Bible shows us that in the chaotic moments—as
well as the peaceful moments—we have a shelter available
to us that will shield us from fear, stress, despair and whatever else we come up against at any moment.

In the Bible, God is often described as "our strong
tower" or "our covering." If we just stop, even for a few seconds, and close our eyes to consider that our God is a shelter from all adversity and a strong, protective father who is

always on our side, we can relax and find a few seconds of solitude and peace.

It is important to have moments like this to focus on God, to find a secret place with Him, where the things of this world fall away. We can then move back out into the crazy flow of our lives, still sensing and knowing that we're in God's shelter, working with the peace and confidence of being covered by Him. As the psalmist writes, "He will cover you with his feathers, and under his wings you will find refuge" (Psalm 91:4).

The music business often thrives on chaos. I tend to have a cycle of seasons of long days of chaos followed by short periods of normality. During the busy seasons, I sometimes get to a place where I can't see the end of the tunnel and feel badgered on many sides by demands from clients, family and church.

It is easy for me to succumb to frustration or despair when I have more tasks in front of me than I can handle or have tasks I don't enjoy doing. However, I can usually find a moment in the madness to excuse myself and have a moment to ask God to show me to His secret place.

Life in our productive years is often a whirlwind of commitments, responsibilities and deadlines. I believe it has been this way for thousands of years. God knows we need peace, and He offers Himself as a sanctuary. We only need to step in.

POINT TO PONDER

GOD IS A REFUGE AVAILABLE TO US IN THE
MIDST OF ANY SURROUNDINGS.

QUESTIONS TO CONSIDER

1. When life starts to go really fast and everything feels out of control, do you access the rich refuge of God? How might you build this into your daily schedule?

2. Do you have a physical location at work or at home where you can seek refuge?

3. Think about what it means to say that God is your protector, your covering, your strong tower. How can this help you sort through the craziness of work? How can this help you to prioritize your days?

DISPLAYING CHRISTLIKE BEHAVIOR IN THE BOARDROOM

ALLISON FLEXER

DIRECTOR OF FINANCIAL AND OPERATIONAL ANALYSIS, MEDTEL INTERNATIONAL

8

Everyone should be quick to listen, slow to speak and slow to become angry, for man's anger does not bring about the righteous life that God desires.

JAMES 1:19-20

When I think of the things that hinder productive business meetings and impair teamwork among colleagues in corporations, it strikes me that these hindrances are often the same sins that the Bible cautions us against displaying.

How many times have we allowed pride to keep us from sharing ideas with team members? Displayed anger when our ideas were rejected for better solutions? Demanded that others listen to us when we should be listening to the counsel of those around us? Or not accepted responsibility for failing to complete a task, solve a problem or meet the budget—in other words, shifting the blame?

Our behavior as business professionals can lead others toward Christ or drive them away. James 1:19-20 states that we should "be quick to listen [and] slow to speak." Can you imagine how much more we might learn as managers if we followed this advice and listened more and spoke less? In this same passage, James also implores us to be "slow to become angry." How many times has our anger provided a source of negative motivation to employees?

As I strive to be a valued team member and a respected manager within my company, I have found the Bible to be an applicable guide along that path. I have also discovered that reflecting on passages of Scripture before attending a meeting can bring me a sense of humility. It encourages me to set aside my own agenda so that I can listen and learn from my team members.

Sometimes, it's difficult for me to apply these biblical principles and "deny myself" in the business world, especially when that world encourages me to look out for myself and climb the corporate ladder—regardless of whether that involves stepping on others along the way. When these corporate tendencies cloud my judgment, I try to picture Jesus as the CEO of a company. What values would He want His employees to embody? It's likely that Jesus would want His employees to value the same things that we find throughout the Scriptures—the values that can guide us to behave in a way that leads our coworkers toward Christ.

POINT TO PONDER

IS JESUS THE CEO OF YOUR PERSONAL LIFE
AND YOUR CORPORATE LIFE?

QUESTIONS TO CONSIDER

1. When you are at work, are you "quick to listen, slow to speak and slow to become angry"? How can you put these principles into action?

2. Are you a good example for Christ in your workplace? Why or why not? What hinders you from being a Christlike example at work?

3. Is the Bible an applicable guide in your life at work? How do you think Jesus would work if He had your job?

Have You Prayed for It?

Gary Layne

PRESIDENT, THE PERFECT CLONE, INC.
COMPUTER CONSULTING FIRM

9

When you ask, you do not receive, because you ask with wrong motives,
that you may spend what you get on your pleasures.

JAMES 4:3

After Hurricane Katrina devastated the Mississippi Gulf Coast, our church sent some teams to Biloxi, Mississippi, to help. I was driving the van with 14 other men who, like me, had no idea how terrible the conditions would be or what we would encounter. We just knew we had to help, so that was what we planned to do.

We loaded what we thought would be the most needed supplies and had them driven down in another truck. Every person in the vehicle was a businessman who knew how to handle tough situations at work. Yet even before we got to the church site, we were stunned by what we saw. Boats were on top of houses, houses were on top of cars, and cars were stuck in treetops. We drove through a neighborhood that had nothing but piles of debris where houses once stood. We were out of our league, totally beyond what we could handle in a weeklong trip. This would take years!

I was responsible for the team that was handing out food, water and cleaning supplies. Each day, we encountered more than 700 families that needed food and water. There was no way we would have enough supplies. The local stores were mostly closed or destroyed. It seemed to be a lost cause. I called my team members together and commented that only God was going to be able to do this. We needed to stop and pray for everything. Not just *some* things, but for *everything*.

We learned a very valuable lesson about God and prayer. *Be specific*. When we needed rice, we prayed for rice and received Rice Krispies cereal. When we prayed for 50-pound bags of white rice, that is what we received. When we prayed for toilet paper we got some—about 10 rolls. When we prayed for an entire truckload of supplies to last through the whole day, God provided it. I could go on and on.

We learned from the experience that we must trust God for everything, pray specifically and pray expectantly. I left my job and have worked at the same church in Biloxi for more than eight months now. God has met every need that we have had. Every one!

POINT TO PONDER

THE BIBLE SAYS THAT WE HAVE NOT BECAUSE WE ASK NOT
OR BECAUSE WE ASK WITH THE WRONG MOTIVES.

QUESTIONS TO CONSIDER

1. How specific are you when you pray for something in your life? What kinds of things do you need right now? Be as specific as possible.

2. Do you ever pray just to praise and thank God for His blessings? Put aside all your requests, your expectant prayers and your petitions and just praise God right now for His blessings.

3. When God answers your prayers or blesses you in specific ways, do you tell others about it? Tell your friends and loved ones about a specific answer to prayer today.

Turning Evil
to Good

David Friedman

Senior Consultant, Oxford Analytica

10

He is like a tree planted by streams of water, which yields its fruit in season and whose leaf does not wither. Whatever he does prospers.

PSALM 1:3

Joseph's life was one filled with wrongful accusations and betrayals. He was betrayed by his brothers, falsely accused by his master's wife, thrown into prison and left to languish there for years. Yet when Joseph surveyed his circumstances, he was able to proclaim with boldness that what others meant for evil, God had used for good:

> You intended to harm me, but God intended it for good to accomplish what is now being done, the saving of many lives. So then, don't be afraid. I will provide for you and your children (Genesis 50:20-21).

This can be as true for us in our lives and careers as it was for Joseph. As a young man, Joseph did not yet have the character to sustain the destiny that God had revealed to him through his dreams. But the history of God's remedy for Joseph's character gap surfaces a key principle: Prosperity and promotion in his life and career came through a constant decision to trust God and serve those around him in humility.

God has to take us through circumstances that will wean us off of acting in the flesh so that He can move us to act out of His Spirit. God uses our careers to test where our identities and trust are really rooted. We should thus embrace those difficult coworkers or situations that God places in our life as His crucible for character growth so that He can position us for His abundance.

I once managed a project with a team member who was one of the most difficult individuals with whom I have ever worked. I decided to obey the words of 1 Peter 3:8-9, which states:

Finally, all of you, live in harmony with one another; be sympathetic, love as brothers, be compassionate and humble. Do not repay evil with evil or insult with insult, but with blessing, because to this you were called so that you may inherit a blessing.

I served this individual and prayed for God's blessing on him and, as it turned out, God used the situation to open the door for a whole new chapter in my career. If you walk in love, God will turn your circumstances around.

Despite the betrayal and backstabbing that Joseph endured, the Lord was always with Joseph, and he prospered. God had promised greatness for Joseph, yet even though he found himself working for a prison guard and condemned with a baker and a cupbearer, he chose to serve those around him. This provided the window for God to turn around his situation.

In the end, Joseph was released from prison for interpreting the pharaoh's dreams. At the age of 30, he was put in charge of the whole land of Egypt and was second only to the pharaoh. By this time, Joseph had the character to leverage the information that God had revealed through Pharaoh's dream.

God gave Joseph wisdom on the future trends in the grain markets that allowed him to both prosper and later save the country. In essence, he was the first grain futures trader. Ultimately, there would be enough food to feed his family when they arrived and, in particular, his brother Judah, who was carrying the line of Christ.

This Joseph Principle can work for each of us: Choose to serve and God will open the door and turn evil circumstances to good in your life and career.

POINT TO PONDER

TRUSTING GOD COMPLETELY AND SERVING OTHERS
IN ANY SITUATION WILL OPEN THE DOOR FOR GOD TO
BLESS US WITH NEW OPPORTUNITIES.

QUESTIONS TO CONSIDER

1. Do you feel that your skills and gifts do not fit with your present work situation?

2. What is a simple way for you to live out God's will in your career based on the example of Joseph's life?

3. Does your character line up with your skills? Do you believe that God can prosper you in every situation as He did in Joseph's life?

THE ADVENTURES OF
THE APPRENTICE

JEDD MEDEFIND

DIRECTOR, NATIONAL INITIATIVE IN THE U.S. GOVERNMENT

11

His master replied, "Well done, good and faithful servant!
You have been faithful with a few things; I will put you in charge of
many things. Come and share your master's happiness!"

MATTHEW 25:23

Shortly after college, three close friends and I headed out to
live and work with Christians across the globe. The journey
offered adventures of a lifetime: forging Russia's frozen north-
land and Nepal's Himalaya, dwelling at a remote mission station in southern Africa, and smuggling Bibles into Vietnam.

But there was also a disappointing element. No matter
how thrilling a place seemed when we arrived, the adrenaline inevitably faded. Even the most exotic places became,
well, somewhat ordinary. We were struck again and again
by the way adventure perennially requires new territory and
crossed edges.

This is true of life in Christ as well. If, as Christians, we feel bored with our faith—and many of us do—it may be because we've stopped moving forward, engaging new territory, or risking anything significant.

Strangely, our travels provided an almost opposite truth as well. As we witnessed the lives of humble Christians in many lands—despite differing languages, cultures and other externals—we observed a bright uniting thread.

There, in the midst of what for these Christians were thoroughly ordinary places, they were living vibrantly in Christ. Despite the repetitiveness and burdens of everyday experiences, they glowed with a purposefulness and vitality we had previously associated only with the exotic and the novel.

Then it struck us: This is the only place where living in Christ can begin. The abundant living that Jesus offers must be found in the pedestrian realities of Monday mornings, or not at all. Of course, God may well call us to far-off lands or daring ventures, but this is rarely the first step.

Now that I've worked for years in more ordinary settings, the common thread present among those vibrant believers has come into greater focus for me. In a word, they live as apprentices to Jesus. He is not merely "their" ticket into heaven but also the Master . . . the expert . . . the maestro. They give the same kind of attention to replicating His ways that a young painter would give to Michelangelo or a golfer would

51

give to Tiger Woods. They truly affirm:

> If anyone obeys his word, God's love is truly made complete in him. This is how we know we are in him: Whoever claims to live in Him must walk as Jesus did (1 John 2:5-6).

For me, pursuing apprenticeship has meant re-exploring the Gospels to examine how Jesus would approach activities central to my daily work, especially communication. The things I've observed—Jesus' deep attentiveness, particularly to those on the margins; the way He met people in terms familiar to them; His ubiquitous asking of questions—have roused fresh amazement at the ways of the Master.

These are concrete ways to walk as Jesus did amidst daily life. Actions such as these rarely bring tingly emotions or an adrenaline rush, but they do add vigor and purpose to every Monday morning.

This is where the commonplace and the novel, the ordinary and the unordinary—the edges—intersect. It is when we daily approach the Master, observe His ways, and then act on what we see. Such a life begins in the ordinary places but leads to adventures that can't be found anywhere else.

POINT TO PONDER

APPRENTICESHIP TO JESUS AMIDST LIFE'S MOST ORDINARY
MOMENTS IS WHERE THE ADVENTURE OF FAITH BEGINS.

QUESTIONS TO CONSIDER

1. In what specific ways are you trying to live as if you were an apprentice to Jesus in the small and seemingly ordinary things of daily life?

2. Pick one of the Gospels (Matthew, Mark, Luke or John) and take the time to read through four or five chapters. What qualities do you see Jesus modeling in the passage you chose?

3. Ask God to give you His qualities today. How do you think being and acting more like Jesus will turn your life into an adventure?

REMEMBER WHO
YOU ARE AND WHOM
YOU REPRESENT

FORMER EXECUTIVE VICE PRESIDENT, CISCO SYSTEMS

12

The king's heart is in the hand of the LORD; he directs it like
a watercourse wherever he pleases.

PROVERBS 21:1

Who we deem as important is often evident by our con-
duct. As Christians, we proclaim to be followers of Christ
and that He is God. This means we are to recognize that He
alone is all-powerful, all-knowing and all-seeing. In fact,
His capabilities and attributes are beyond comparison and
beyond our comprehension.

Further, we enjoy a personal relationship with God and
have access to Him 24/7 without appointment or having to
go through staff managers, executive assistants, secretaries
or any other gatekeepers. We can go to Him directly and do

not have to justify why we need to speak with Him. Yet perhaps it is this ease of accessibility that subliminally feeds our forgetfulness of Who it is that we know and just how important He is. When we are feeling intimidated in the presence of another human being, we must question both our recognition of these things and our reasoning.

It is fascinating to me how people will feel intimidated in the presence of someone they regard as talented, bright or powerful. They will worry and fret whether their remarks will be viewed with favor or whether their request will be granted. They fear that a question will be asked that they cannot answer. They perceive that a project approval, a new order, or perhaps even career advancement hangs in the balance of this one important person's response to their petition.

Meetings such as these are best handled by first concentrating on Christ. After all, "The king's heart is in the hand of the LORD; he directs it like a watercourse wherever he pleases" (Proverbs 21:1). In addition, "He changes times and seasons; he sets up kings and deposes them. He gives wisdom to the wise and knowledge to the discerning" (Daniel 2:21). All we need to do is pray, prepare and then trust God for the right outcome. He ultimately controls the results of the meeting and determines who has authority in it.

Jesus is not waiting for an appointment to see the CEO of GM, IBM or even the president of the United States. He is not in need of their approval or wisdom. They, just like you and I, are in need of His approval. And do you know what? You know Him! So next time, remember who you are and Whom you represent!

POINT TO PONDER

YOU HAVE INSTANTANEOUS ACCESS TO GOD ALMIGHTY, THE HIGHEST AND MOST POWERFUL AUTHORITY.

QUESTIONS TO CONSIDER

1. What business executive is important enough in your life to cause a feeling of intimidation? Is your feeling of intimidation warranted?

2. In those moments when you feel intimidated, how can you combat the feelings of insecurity or doubt?

3. Do you ever find that you intimidate others? If so, do you remember to act in a way that is representative of Jesus Christ?

PUBLIC RELATIONS

KEVON SABER

VICE PRESIDENT OF SALES AND MARKETING
AND COFOUNDER, GENPLAY GAMES

13

My sheep listen to my voice; I know them, and they follow me.
I give them eternal life, and they shall never perish;
no one can snatch them out of my hand.

JOHN 10:27-28

As a young entrepreneur, I wanted to reduce any doubts my coworkers might have about me due to my youth. So I decided to be an example of professionalism, efficiency and discipline and started arriving at the office hours before my coworkers would show up. As everyone was arriving, I made a point of being in my office, which was located near the front door, from 8:30 A.M. until 9:30 A.M.

One morning at 8:00 A.M., my friend called and said, "I need to meet with you right now." He was facing some personal challenges. Sensing the urgency in his voice, I asked him if he could hold on for a minute. Putting the phone down, I prayed, "God, what should I do?"

I felt strongly that God wanted me to spend some time with my friend, but my self-imposed corporate routine made it difficult for me to leave my desk and take the time to meet with him. Then I had an idea: I could meet with him in the conference room that also happened to be near the door.

One by one, my associates walked in. It seemed that many of them looked puzzled to see me, "Mr. Efficiency," meeting with a friend at work. After meeting with him for about 25 minutes, we heard a surprising knock on the door. Our customer service manager walked into the conference room to tell me that a producer from the Bay Area CBS affiliate wanted to know if I could do a live interview on television the following morning.

At first I chuckled on the inside, and then I laughed heartily aloud. God handed us a sizeable media hit while I was managing my reputation in a paranoid manner inside our company. I felt a little bit like Peter and John after they cast their net on the right side of the boat (see John 21:4-6).

Through this situation at work, God taught me that He will help me to succeed and that I don't need to manage the minutiae. He also reinforced my need to surrender all of my time (even my office time) to Him. I almost sacrificed being obedient and missing an opportunity to bless my friend because I had conditioned myself not to do anything personal on the job.

POINT TO PONDER

IF JESUS ISN'T THE LORD OF ALL,
HE'S NOT LORD AT ALL.

QUESTIONS TO CONSIDER

1. When opportunities to serve people conflict with corporate norms or your work routine, how do you decide what to do?

2. Can you listen to God's voice while you're in your work environment? What sorts of distractions or factors get in the way of you hearing from God in this way?

3. How can you be more sensitive to God's voice in your work environment?

A QUESTION OF TRUST

BILLY LEONARD

PRODUCTION MANAGER, OVERSEAS RADIO AND TELEVISION

14

*Since you are my rock and my fortress, for the sake of
your name lead and guide me.*

PSALM 31:3

As I picked up the phone to call my CEO's assistant, I still
wondered if I was doing the right thing. There was something
I had to tell my boss that could potentially affect my current
role in the company. This news could cause confusion in the
midst of a major team transition. I was supposed to be head-
ing up a new initiative. The news that I might be leaving would
only serve to disrupt what we were all hoping to accomplish.

In early May, I took the Graduate Management Admis-
sion Test (GMAT), and only recently, I received word via
e-mail that I had scored high on the test. This was one more
confirmation that God was very possibly leading me away
from my current company after four years. Now, the question was how and when to tell this news to my boss.

Common logic—and the common advice I received at the time—said to wait until I actually needed to tell her. I would need to request a recommendation letter in September. Telling her then would still give the company nine months notice to prepare for my departure. But the more I prayed about it, the more I sensed God leading me to tell my boss now. I had developed a relationship with her that was based on honesty, trust and directness.

More important, I felt God telling me that I needed to trust Him in this matter. If I didn't tell my boss now, it would be because I was trying to control the situation. No matter how good my intentions might have been, I believed God wanted me to let go of my role at the company and allow Him to work.

It was a question of trust, and I knew the answer: God did care about the professional projects on which I was working. So, the following day after receiving my official score, I sat down in my CEO's office and told her everything. I asked her to be involved in the process. I asked for her advice. And I did it all more than a year before my possible departure.

Since that meeting, my boss and I have continued to enjoy an honest and direct relationship. Furthermore, she has continued to trust me with the authority necessary to lead the company's two major teams. Most important, the peace I have experienced since that day in her office has confirmed to me that I did the right thing.

Sometimes logic and good intentions can be the enemy of what God is asking me to do. I knew that God had to be in control. I needed Him to be at work, but that could only happen if I placed the transition and my future in His hands.

POINT TO PONDER

TRUST IS A CHOICE, WHICH MUST BE FOLLOWED
BY DIRECT AND INTENTIONAL ACTION.

QUESTIONS TO CONSIDER

1. Do the decisions you make at work—and the resulting actions—reflect a greater trust in God or a greater trust in yourself?

2. Are you comfortable trusting God with the decisions you have to make at work? How can you practice praying over and giving your work decisions to God?

3. What actions would result from your trusting God with a decision you are facing right now? What is keeping you from taking those actions?

TECHNOLOGY: THE NEW AMERICAN IDOL

GABE KNAPP

SENIOR PRODUCT MANAGER, MICROSOFT CORPORATION

15

Be still, and know that I am God; I will be exalted among
the nations, I will be exalted in the earth.

PSALM 46:10

It's amazing! With my new cell phone, I can send and receive
e-mails from anywhere, surf the web or even listen to music or
watch a movie. Never before has it been possible for me to be so
productive or so entertained regardless of where I am—and all
thanks to a beautiful little device that fits neatly in my pocket.

Whether it's a cell phone, PC or an iPod, high tech gadg-
ets are playing a greater role in our lives than ever before.
There's no question that innovations in technology offer us
many new conveniences and provide us with many benefits.
However, I've recently found that sometimes my prayer life
suffers as a result of all this technology.

E-mail, text messaging and voicemail—even digital enter-tainment—make it all too easy for me to fill the gaps in my work day by cranking out another e-mail response or turning to my device to receive my next instruction. Whether I'm on vacation or just on the go, it's tempting to jump on the Internet or reach for a device. When I go jogging, I grab my portable music player. On a plane, I watch a DVD movie. When I jump in the car, I automatically reach for the stereo.

The reality is that while technology offers us increased convenience, it can also consume our time and thoughts. The Bible tells us that God is a jealous God. He desires a close relationship with us and wants to spend time with us to know our deepest thoughts. Psalm 46:10 says:

> Be still, and know that I am God;
> I will be exalted among the nations,
> I will be exalted in the earth.

When was the last time we were able to take time out of our hectic workday to just "be still"?

Technology makes our lives much easier, but we must be careful that the time we spend with technology does not replace our daily time with God. We need to seek direction from God, not from the new e-mail in our inbox. We need to worship Jesus Christ, not the latest technology.

POINT TO PONDER

AM I BEING INTENTIONAL ABOUT SPENDING DAILY TIME WITH GOD?

QUESTIONS TO CONSIDER

1. Do you find that technology ever interferes with your time with God? Do you have healthy boundaries in place at work and at home that make room for God in your life?

2. What does it mean to "be still" and listen for God's voice? Will you commit to turning off your electronic devices for part of the day and trying it?

3. Do you find yourself more likely to turn to God for direction or to technology? How can you use technology to get *closer* to God?

Busy for God

Katie McNerney
Marketing Manager, eBay, Inc.

16

*For it is by grace you have been saved, through faith—and this
not from yourselves, it is the gift of God.*

Ephesians 2:8

Most people would call me an overachiever, a label that for
me has generally positive connotations. I enjoy staying busy.
It makes me feel productive. Being productive also often
translates into accomplishing goals, which typically lead to
some kind of reward. It's an appealing cycle, and one that
I've practiced much of my life.

In my life, I have found that the benefits of being an
overachiever have typically outweighed the disadvantages.
The pleasure I have taken in accomplishing a goal usually
has trumped the long days and sleepless nights. Throughout
my life, I have been rewarded (at least in the worldly sense)
for my accomplishments. Whether it was praise from my

parents, acceptance by teachers, or wins on the soccer field, my achievements always seemed to translate into the value I offered to the world. In turn, I overbooked my schedule with activities in order to stay busy, and therefore productive.

One February morning a few years ago, I achieved the pinnacle of my goals when I was accepted into one of the country's top business schools. At the time, I couldn't imagine a more perfect reward for all my hard work. To top it off, I was engaged to a wonderful man, and we were busy preparing for our wedding.

My life looked pretty amazing, clearly the result of a lifetime of hard work (or so I told myself). Not one month later, however, the perfect little world I had worked so hard to build suddenly fell apart. My fiancé died of a heart arrhythmia. I remember waking up the next morning wondering how I could be in this place after all I had accomplished in my life.

It has taken a while for me to realize that my destructive pattern of motivation came from an insecurity of wanting to prove my significance to the world. And, yes, I've even been tempted to work hard at fixing *that*. The good news is that we don't have to fix ourselves, because God has already done the work for us.

In Ephesians 2:8, Paul reminds us that it is by grace we have been saved, not by works. God wants us to work, use the gifts he has given us and not stand idle, but we must remember that we do this work not because it will save us but because we are already saved. Our motivation for work must be gratitude and praise for God's mercy. "For we are God's workmanship, created in Christ Jesus to do good works" (v. 10).

POINT TO PONDER

No accomplishment or act we can do will save us. It is only through God's grace that we are saved.

QUESTIONS TO CONSIDER

1. Do you attempt to achieve goals just to achieve them? Does achieving a goal sometimes feel more important than the reason for achieving that goal?

2. When you analyze your work habits and your schedule, what do you find truly motivates your actions every day?

3. Where do you find your worth and significance as a person? Is it found in the things you achieve or in God's love for you?

APPROACHING THE TEMPLE

PAT GELSINGER

SENIOR VICE PRESIDENT, GENERAL MANAGER OF
DIGITAL ENTERPRISE GROUP, INTEL CORPORATION

*When I saw him, I fell at his feet as though dead. Then he placed his right
hand on me and said: "Do not be afraid. I am the First and the Last."*

REVELATION 1:17

I've visited Israel on quite a few occasions during my years
with Intel and have been to the Holy City of Jerusalem a
number of times. However, on a recent trip, a guide told me
something I had never heard before.

In the days of Temple worship, the Israelites would have
climbed stairs up to the Temple Mount before entering the
courtyard to present their sacrifice. The Temple Mount
itself was an extremely large area. On a special occasion such
as Passover, there might be as many as several hundreds of
thousands of visitors in a single day. Each of those visitors
would have made the climb up that long, massive staircase
to the Temple of the almighty God.

Why would God create this stairway leading up to the Temple mount? Why do you think He would have designed such an arduous climb into the weekly worship ritual? Imagine coming into the very presence of God as you climb those stairs:

- You can't run. You have to walk solemnly and carefully into His presence.

- You can't come with your head raised up. You need to keep your head bowed and reverent as you look carefully at each step.

- You can't be distracted as you come. You need to concentrate carefully each step of the way.

- You can't ride in a cart or on horseback to see God. The only way is to climb the stairs under your own will and strength.

- You can't bring your sacrifice in a cart. You can only sacrifice what you can carry into His presence.

I was struck by the power of the image. Once again, God perfectly accounts for all the details in His plans for

His people to please and worship Him. God seeks each one of us to be Holy as we come to our time of prayer, devotion or weekly worship. While still in our earthly flesh, we need to approach our time with God as if we were entering the throne room, the Holy of Holies, the very presence of God.

POINT TO PONDER

GOD PERFECTLY ACCOUNTS FOR ALL OF THE DETAILS IN ORDER FOR HIS PEOPLE TO PLEASE AND WORSHIP HIM.

QUESTIONS TO CONSIDER

1. How do you approach your time with God, whether you're reading the Scriptures, praying or meditating on the Lord?

2. How do you approach God Himself? Do you ever avoid time with God? Why?

3. What can you apply from this illustration of the Temple stairs to your own time with God?

Seeking God's Kingdom First

Reagan Rylander

Project Manager, Real Estate and
Community Development

18

But seek first his kingdom and his righteousness,
and all these things will be given to you as well.

Matthew 6:33

After being a Christian for more than 15 years, I decided a few years ago that if the Bible is truly the Word of God, I should actually read the whole thing and even memorize a few verses of it. Crazy idea, huh? One of the verses I eventually committed to memory was the above verse in Matthew.

Unfortunately, this verse didn't fit with the way I saw my life working or with what I had learned in business school—or even in church, for that matter. Instead of seeking God's kingdom first, I was actively seeking success, my career, a family and a house. In my mind, after I had achieved sufficient success in this world, I would then be able to flip my priorities and focus on God full time. After all, God helps those who help themselves, right?

However, as I read and reread Scripture during the next few years, I came to the uncomfortable conclusion that my perception of my role as a follower of Christ was really not based on the Bible. Rather, it was based on popular American culture and on theories about what the Bible said. My core belief was that all God required of me was to say a prayer and believe that Jesus died for my sins. Then I could get back to working on building my little kingdom.

When I started digging into the Bible, I saw that Jesus taught His followers that if they didn't follow His example and act on His teachings, they didn't really know Him. He actually spent the majority of His earthly ministry confronting people who smugly thought they were right with God by virtue of their belief system but weren't acting on their faith. Ouch!

One of the things Jesus taught a lot about was money. He talked about people who chased money and success as their god, people who were afraid of losing it or afraid of giving it away, people who stored it up for an uncertain future, and people who were unwilling to use it to transform other people's lives. In fact, on multiple occasions Jesus made a close connection between a person's attitude about money and that person's salvation. Again, ouch!

So, how big a role does money play in your decision-making process?

Maybe money isn't such a tough place to start after all.

G. K. Chesterton once said, "Christianity has not been tried and found lacking; it has been found difficult and left untried." Have you tried it?

POINT TO PONDER

GOD'S KINGDOM MUST BE FIRST IN OUR LIFE.

QUESTIONS TO CONSIDER

1. How much does money control your decisions? Can you think of ways to alter this control?

2. Consider G. K. Chesterton's quote. Do you think what Chesterton says is accurate and that many people don't really try to live the Christian life?

3. How difficult is living out true Christianity? What are some of the factors in your life that contribute to this difficulty?

Is Your Work Sacred or Secular?

Alex Brubaker

MANAGING DIRECTOR, BRUBAKER CONSULTING

19

Each one should use whatever gift he has received to serve others,
faithfully administering God's grace in its various forms.

1 PETER 4:10

As the son of life-long missionaries, I have always felt the tension between the sacred and the secular. I felt this tension most when I was about to graduate from an Ivy League university with highest honors in finance and engineering, and I readied myself to enter the marketplace.

Here I was, a follower of Jesus, feeling conflicted about using a first-rate education in the business world. *What's redeeming about a job in the marketplace if the ultimate objective is only an increased stock price or a better profit margin?* I asked myself. *Would Jesus become a management consultant or investment banker?*

Over the years, I have come to realize that I was operating under a paradigm that segmented all earthly activities into two distinct categories—the *sacred* and the *secular*—and that these categories did not overlap. In this paradigm, working in the marketplace most certainly belonged to the latter category.

It was this same kind of thinking that elevated working in the ministry over working in the marketplace in my own mind (and in the minds of many Christians). Indeed, some believers dissolve the tension between the sacred and the secular by simply becoming pastors or missionaries. I almost did just that. But there is another way to address this tension.

God gives each of us different gifts, passions and callings, and for some of us, these gifts are in the realm of business. If our calling is to advance God's kingdom through business, then that is our highest calling.

Whatever our calling from God—whether in the marketplace or in the Church—our calling is noble and sacred, and the old paradigms fall away. In fact, the sacred and the secular overlap and coexist. Personally, I have found a greater integration of my work (the so-called "secular") and faith (the "sacred") with the realization that I can minister in the marketplace through my business. All aspects of my life, including my work in business, are ministry when they further God's purposes.

I have also come to realize that doing business can be a spiritual activity that has redeeming and sacred value, thereby resolving that age-old tension within Christianity. We need not feel conflicted when we seek to serve God through our work. The marketplace is as legitimate a venue as any other for serving others to the glory of God, and doing so makes our very work a sacred act.

Point to Ponder

All work that honors God and fulfills His calling is sacred, including serving others through business.

Questions to Consider

1. What are the redeeming aspects of your work? What makes your work sacred?

2. How can your business activity, or your job, be considered a spiritual activity? Do you truly believe that business can be a spiritual activity that has redeeming value?

3. Do you ever feel the tension between work and your ministry or your calling from God? Could it be that these things are bound together?

The Pit Stop

Rodney Gibson IV
Director, Archstone-Smith

20

Keep my Sabbaths as holy rest days, signposts between me and you,
signaling that I am God, your God.
Ezekiel 20:20, *The Message*

Racing is a sport I know very little about, yet it captures my attention every time I see a race. Formula One, NASCAR and other racing circuits all display man's innate desire for speed, hard work and efficiency.

As one who is sometimes guilty of a heavy foot on back-stretches of the highway, I love the sensory assault of the race track: the roar of the motors, the smells of the cars screaming past performing at their peak, and watching a driver testing the limits of his or her driving ability.

Many of us do the same with our professional careers—we're eternally locked into a daily routine, striving for the next deal, the next bonus or the next promotion. But there is at least one major difference between life on the track as a racecar driver and life as a businessperson. That difference is the pit stop.

Even though racecars are true feats of engineering, their parts wear down, their fuel runs low and their drivers need an occasional break. What a strange concept: In a sport that involves speeds in excess of 200 mph, it is essential to come to a complete stop multiple times during competition in order to win.

However, these kinds of regularly scheduled breaks do not seem to be a part of corporate life, especially with the recent advent of working lunches and client meetings disguised as coffee breaks. Car racing, on the other hand, builds the pit stop into its very format *because it's totally necessary*.

Other sports incorporate the same principle. In football, soccer and basketball, the players stop and take a needed break during halftime. In baseball, this break is known as the seventh-inning stretch. Even cricket—in which matches can last for days—have formal intervals for lunch and tea (and shorter breaks when necessary).

These traditions are a part of sports because they're necessary and healthy for the athletes involved. In addition, the concept of tapering—strategic rest and recovery before key competition—is foreign to the office, although sports coaches around the world require their athletes to rest before key competitions.

God even made rest a part of His own schedule when He created the earth:

> By the seventh day God had finished the work he had been doing; so on the seventh day he rested from all his work. And God blessed the seventh day and made it holy, because on it he rested from all the work of creating that he had done (Genesis 2:2-3).

We see this theme repeated throughout the Scriptures. In fact, one of the Ten Commandments that Moses gave to the Israelites related to the Sabbath day of rest:

> Remember the Sabbath day by keeping it holy. Six days you shall labor and do all your work, but the seventh day is a Sabbath to the Lord your God. On it you shall not do any work (Exodus 20:8-10).

So it is clear that without a pit stop of any kind, optimal performance is difficult to achieve. Therefore, as business people we should consider building strategic rest and recovery, along with regular breaks, into the "corporate" competition.

On this day, the Sabbath, we are called by God to enter into His rest.

POINT TO PONDER

GOD CALLS US TO MORE THAN
50 DAYS OF MANDATED HOLIDAY EACH YEAR.
WHO WOULDN'T WANT TO TAKE IT?

QUESTIONS TO CONSIDER

1. Do you enjoy a Sabbath day—a day each week when you just kick back and rest?

2. If you do not do this, how much more effective do you think you would be at work if you really did enjoy a day of Sabbath rest each week?

3. Mark 2:27 states, "The Sabbath was made to serve us; we weren't made to serve the Sabbath." What do you think this phrase means?

Acknowledging Faith in the Workplace

Jon Venverloh

Strategic Partnerships, Google

21

Whoever acknowledges me before men, I will also
acknowledge him before my Father in heaven.

MATTHEW 10:32

In many areas of the country, and particularly the San Francisco Bay Area that I call home, the culture of political correctness and multiculturalism frowns on any favorable mention of the God of the Bible.

Submitting to God and the decrees of His Word are contrary to the prevailing secular humanist mind-set in which the individual is esteemed above all and God is perceived as a fairy tale or as an opiate for the masses. In the workplace, reliance on God is often seen as irrational, non-intellectual and perhaps even irresponsible.

Google, my employer, has its origin in academia and retains incredibly bright, high-performance people. A lot of brilliant minds are hard at work in the Googleplex, where the culture is dominated by computer science and where scientifically observable proof is highly valued. For many, this culture leaves no room for matters of faith.

Of course, Google is not unusual among Silicon Valley tech companies. Many workplace cultures are ambivalent and even hostile toward religion in general and Christianity in particular. So as a Christian, I pray and ask God regularly how I can best honor Him in the workplace. But I must confess that I have often feared that my faith will perhaps alienate my peers and superiors.

What does God want from us in the workplace? As in other contexts, He calls us out of the mainstream to a different standard—one of holiness:

> Therefore come out from them and be separate, says the Lord. Touch no unclean thing, and I will receive you (2 Corinthians 6:17).

Jesus promises to bless us if we honor Him publicly with our words and actions:

> Whoever acknowledges me before men, I will also acknowledge him before my Father in heaven (Matthew 10:32).

Finally, His Word calls us to exemplify integrity to non-believers:

> Live such good lives among the pagans that, though they accuse you of doing wrong, they may see your good deeds and glorify God on the day he visits us (1 Peter 2:12).

I believe God wants to bless those who believe in Him. In the context of the workplace, "blessing" usually means success in our work and perhaps career advancement (though not always, as sometimes He has something different and better in store). Regardless of my specific circumstances at any given time, I want God to approve of what I am doing. For if He is with me, who can be against me?

I want to honor the Lord in my workplace, being faithful to my employer through exceptional performance. I want to glorify the Lord through sanctioned forums such as a workplace Bible study or lunchtime fellowship meetings.

It is my prayer that the Lord will show me opportunities each day to share with my coworkers that I believe God is to be thanked for the abundant life we lead. For the Lord truly can bless the work of our hands and let our words and actions glorify Him, not just at home or at church, but also at work.

POINT TO PONDER

OUR FAITH WILL BE TESTED WHEN WE SEEK TO GIVE GLORY TO
GOD INSTEAD OF TO OURSELVES IN THE WORKPLACE.

QUESTIONS TO CONSIDER

1. What can you do today to glorify God at your specific place of business?

2. Do you think God can use you to glorify Him even in a place where talking about what God has done in your life might feel uncomfortable?

3. Do you think you can live in such a way that everyone will glorify God on the day He returns, as it says in 1 Peter 2:12?

THE MARCH OF OBEDIENCE

ALLEN WOLF

PRESIDENT, MORNING STAR PICTURES AND MORNING STAR GAMES

22

> *Joshua went up to him and asked, "Are you for us or for our enemies?" "Neither," he replied, "but as commander of the army of the LORD I have now come."*
>
> JOSHUA 5:13-14

I frequently ask God the same question as Joshua: "Are You for me, God?" I tell Him that I'm working hard to glorify Him through my business, my decisions and my time. Yet His answer is always a resounding no. God is for Himself.

In fact, by asking God if He is for me, I realize that I am asking the wrong question. The better question would be, "Am *I* for God?" God is never going to follow what I'm doing, but I can follow what God is doing.

Shortly after Joshua had this encounter with the "commander of the army of the Lord," he was commanded to have his army march around the walls of Jericho, blowing their trumpets for seven days. On the seventh day, he was to tell the Israelites to shout, and the walls of Jericho would fall down. What God was calling Joshua's army to do seemed absurd. What does parading around a city and shouting have to do with walls collapsing?

The life God calls us to live often seems similar to that absurd command. God calls us to obey Him when it's not convenient, to spend time reading His Scripture when we already feel crushed by all our other responsibilities, and to pray when the answers are often difficult to see. It's as if we are being commanded to shout our prayers and march in obedience while life's obstacles continue to loom over us.

When Joshua told the Israelites to shout on the seventh day of their absurd march, I imagine they started shouting timidly at first. But as they saw the walls buckle and the giant stone walls collapse, I'm sure that their timid yelling transformed into victorious shouts. In the same way, when I forge ahead in the march of obedience God has given me, I also see walls crack and tumble. Sometimes, those walls are around my heart, sometimes they are in my business, and sometimes in my relationships or a new area of my life the Lord wants to claim as His own.

When I feel drained or start to forget why I'm marching, I have to return to the commander of the army of the Lord.

His sword is always drawn. It is His battle to win.

I can shout and march around the walls of my life if I trust in God's timing. He'll make the walls come down when He's ready. I just need to remind myself that I follow the victorious King of kings who will stop at nothing to claim every area of my life as His own. All I have to do is follow His commands and pursue Him wherever He leads.

POINT TO PONDER

GOD IS CALLING US TO OBEY HIM DESPITE OUR CIRCUMSTANCES.

QUESTIONS TO CONSIDER

1. In what areas of your life are you resisting God's call to obedience? What will you commit to do in order to change this pattern of behavior?

2. Do you ever feel as if God is asking you to do something foolish or downright silly? Do you think He might be seeking to bless you in that situation?

3. If God is for Himself, how might that change your priorities if you realign them to God's priorities?

The "Five Whys" of God's Economy

Rachel Carriere

SENIOR ASSOCIATE, POINT B SOLUTIONS GROUP, LLP

23

*Why are you downcast, O my soul? Why so disturbed within me? Put your
hope in God, for I will yet praise him, my Savior and my God.*

PSALM 42:5-6

One of the most memorable cases I studied in business
school was the "Five Whys" problem-solving technique. This
was a technique made popular in the 1970s as part of the
Toyota Production System. It basically involved asking the
question "Why?" up to five times in order to ultimately discover the root cause of any problem.

The basic premise of this method is that whenever the
personnel at Toyota encountered a difficulty or problem,
they could ask five questions as to why the particular com-
plication occurred. The management team at the car company found that by using this method, most problems could be

resolved. One question would lead to another, which led to another, and then to another—until one question ultimately got to the true cause of the problem.

This approach resonated with my analytical mind and interest in problem solving. However, while I found that this is a very effective technique in the business world, I have learned that it does not apply to my walk with Christ. Not every question in life can be answered by simply asking why something occurred.

When I do not understand events in my own life, I often find myself asking "Why?" and engaging my analytical mind. For example, a few years ago, I encountered a health issue that perplexed my doctors. Every medical test performed on me came back normal, and the doctors did not know why I was not feeling well.

My tendency was to keep asking "Why?" in an attempt to find the root cause. Yet after continually pursuing answers and repeatedly hearing the doctors say, "I don't know," I realized that God wanted me to stop asking why and rely on Him. He knew the entire situation, including my frustration, and I needed to just have faith in His plan for my life.

After enduring a year of many medical tests and not finding an answer, the doctors eventually diagnosed a rather benign condition. I can now say that I am extremely grateful for this time of uncertainty in my life.

Now, my faith is stronger and I've learned how God wants me to answer the confusing situations that arise in my personal life: Have faith and trust in God's understanding.

POINT TO PONDER

GOD'S UNDERSTANDING SURPASSES OUR OWN UNDERSTANDING. WE NEED TO TRUST THAT HE HAS AN AMAZING PLAN FOR OUR LIVES.

QUESTIONS TO CONSIDER

1. Do you try to apply the "Five Whys" or some other analytical process to your life and walk with God? Do you find that it is effective?

2. Are you able to trust in God's understanding and not your own? Why or why not?

3. How can a process such as the "Five Whys"—while productive in many situations—ultimately counteract God's holy plan for your life?

You're Not in Control

Todd Barr

Marketing, Red Hat

24

Wealth and honor come from you; you are the ruler of all things.
In your hands are strength and power to exalt and give strength to all.

1 Chronicles 29:12

There's a guy who sits in the cubicle next to me who always comes over and interrupts me. In fact, this same type of guy has been in the cube next to me at every job I've ever had. There's probably one that sits next to you, too.

You know the type of guy I'm talking about—he's the one who comes around the corner, leans down and says, "Did you hear about Jones? He just got a promotion. I've been here three years, and I haven't received a promotion. What's the deal?"

Or sometimes, he says, "Hey, did you see that Human Resources just posted a new director job? I know I have no experience in that area, but I'm not going anywhere in this job. Should I apply for it?"

Or, on particularly bad days, he barges in with, "I hate this place. I bust my tail for this company and I'm not appreciated. You know, I just saw this great job posted on Monster.com. Maybe I should apply." You know this guy, don't you? I know him well . . . in fact, sometimes *I am* that guy.

Living this way is similar to riding a roller coaster. Sure, there are moments of glee when you get a promotion or seize an opportunity, but most of your time is spent in fear and uncertainty about whether or not your career is going as you planned it. You are consumed with thoughts such as, *Am I getting paid enough? Am I moving up fast enough? Should I look for another job? Why did he get promoted and I didn't?* And whenever you are in a particularly low point, Monster.com becomes a hopeful haven.

The good news is that it doesn't have to be this way. Living in fear is not the life that God wants for you. I have found great comfort and freedom in realizing that while I am not in control, there is a loving and caring God who is.

In 1 Chronicles 29:12, David says, "Wealth and honor come from you; you are the ruler of all things. In your hands are strength and power to exalt and give strength to all."

The key phrases in which I take comfort in these verses are "you are the ruler of all things" and "in your hands are strength and power to exalt and give strength to all." It is not up to me whether or not I get promoted; it is up to God. It is not up to me if I get wealth or honor; it is up to God. When I remember that He is in control, I am free to focus on what He is trying to teach me now, in my present position, and to be open to His leading when He provides new opportunities.

POINT TO PONDER

THERE IS FREEDOM IN KNOWING THAT GOD
IS IN CONTROL OF OUR CAREERS.

QUESTIONS TO CONSIDER

1. Are you consumed with always looking out for that next promotion or that next job opportunity? What is the danger in living your life in this manner?

2. How can you give up control and take hold of God's freedom to overcome unhealthy ambition?

3. If God alone has the ability to exalt and give strength to all, then all the factors we think determine those who are exalted mean nothing. What factors *are* meaningful?

THE POWER OF PRAYER

VIRENDRA VASE

GENERAL MANAGEMENT, EXPERIAN

25

Be joyful always; pray continually; give thanks in all circumstances,
for this is God's will for you in Christ Jesus.

1 THESSALONIANS 5:16-18

Most of us feel a bit guilty when it comes to the amount of time we spend with God. I am no exception to this generalization. Having said that, I have not given up on praying for my coworkers.

Not too long ago, I was in a Business as Ministry Bible study, and the topic was "Miracles in the Marketplace." Like most people, I doubted the possibility of miracles occurring in Silicon Valley. However, I prayed and asked the Lord to provide a miracle.

That week, I met with one of my coworkers for our regularly scheduled one-on-one times, expecting to go through the normal business-related issues. However, before I could open my mouth, she asked me, "How can I know more about Jesus?"

I almost fainted because, honestly, she was the last person I would have expected to ask me that question. I could not believe it was really happening. I figured that this only happened to other people, not me.

During the following weeks, I continued to answer her questions and pray for her, and God continued to remind me to have faith as a mustard seed:

96

> If you have faith as small as a mustard seed, you can say to this mulberry tree, "Be uprooted and planted in the sea," and it will obey you (Luke 17:6).

To make a long story short, my coworker accepted the Lord Jesus a few months later and today is serving the Lord with all her heart and soul. Although God used me (among other people), He was already at work in this person's life.

What did the Lord teach me through this experience? To never give up and to always keep praying. Moreover, He taught me to continue to be the "salt and light" that He has asked me to be in the business world (see Matthew 5:13-14).

Today, I know that God will continue to use me right where I am.

Point to Ponder

God is at work in people's lives. We never know how
He will use us to reach them.

Questions to Consider

1. Have you ever wondered what would happen if you prayed for your coworkers for five minutes each day?

2. Have you ever considered what God would do in your heart if you truly trusted Him to guide you?

3. Is it possible to pray continually? What might that look like?

A Cause for Optimism

FINANCE MANAGEMENT, DELL, INC.

26

We know that in all things God works for the good of those who love him,
who have been called according to his purpose.

ROMANS 8:28

There is a critical leadership trait that even the best MBA programs in the world cannot teach us: having an optimistic attitude in all circumstances.

One week after the birth of my third child, I walked into the vice president's office and told him that the weight of my new job had become unbearable. The only solution that I could see was to resign. After four months of enduring numerous obstacles, unforeseen expectations, ongoing criticism in my new job and many sleepless nights, I was frustrated and ready to quit. Discouragement had turned into disillusionment, then into despair, and finally into depression. I was at an all-time low.

To my surprise, the vice president asked me whether or not I believed in God. He went on to say that as a Christian himself, he did not believe that Christians should be quitters. He suggested that I take the rest of the day off to pray.

After much introspection, I realized that my fall had a lot to do with my pessimistic attitude—one that bred fear and hopelessness during tough circumstances. I had become ineffective around my customers and those whom I was attempting to lead. My faith had become dull, and my attitude had become driven more by self-reliance rather than by the awesome promises of God. As the pressures of life heated up, I had lost faith.

Strong leaders are optimistic. I'm not talking about a pollyanna, superficially positive attitude, but rather one based on the calculated belief that even the toughest of challenges will turn into something good. What we believe affects the way we feel, and how we feel drives how we behave toward others and how we handle problems.

In Romans 8:28, we are reminded that if we love God and seek after His purpose, He causes all things to work together for good. The focus here is that God causes all things to work together—not just in the good times, but also in the tough times. When times are hard or we fail, it's hard to see how that could be "good," but God in His eternal wisdom knows what is good for us.

Through the tough times, God may be maturing our faith in Him, preparing us for bigger challenges, or using us as an example to lead others. With this understanding, we have reason to have an optimistic attitude during every moment of our lives, in every meeting, in every challenge, and in every failure. So, while the vice president's response that day surprised me, it really should not have. After all, God was at work the whole time for my good.

POINT TO PONDER

WE SHOULD HAVE AN OPTIMISTIC ATTITUDE BECAUSE GOD CAUSES ALL THINGS TO WORK TOGETHER FOR GOOD.

QUESTIONS TO CONSIDER

1. How can your attitude change the effectiveness of your work and your relationships with colleagues?
2. Are your mind and attitude driven by God's promises in the Bible or by a false sense of security grounded in self-reliance and spiritual mediocrity?
3. Is your faith in Christ strong enough to endure the toughest business challenges?

POISONOUS IF SWALLOWED

DUANE MOYER

EXECUTIVE VICE PRESIDENT, HIS CHURCH AT WORK

27

*For if you forgive men when they sin against you, your
heavenly Father will also forgive you. But if you do not forgive men
their sins, your Father will not forgive your sins.*

MATTHEW 6:14-15

The label on the side of pesticide bottles expresses the obvious: "Poisonous If Swallowed. Consult a Physician Immediately." Pretty straightforward, but there are poisons that we encounter every day that are far more toxic and carry few, if any, warning labels.

Recently, I learned how easy it is to succumb to the poorly labeled toxins of anger and an unforgiving attitude at work. The poison came from a sequence of unaddressed offenses that went underground and festered in my heart. At first, I pretended I wasn't really hurt, but after a few months it became clear that I had been hurt and was holding unresolved anger.

Unfortunately, I processed my anger by talking about my offender with others, which only fueled justification for my anger. I also took my case of injustice to God by complaining and crying foul. I ended up creating mistrust among my team toward my offender. My personal productivity, along with the whole team, began to deteriorate.

Eventually, my slanderous talk surfaced and caused a major blowout that led to my leaving the company. Dumbfounded and disillusioned, I cried out to God, and He allowed me to see my lack of forgiveness through the megaphone of the pain of my unemployment.

At the very root of my unwillingness to forgive was pride. Pride, because I didn't trust God to take care of me, and pride because I was demanding immediate justice from my offender. The reason God says that we are to forgive others in order for Him to forgive us is because we must trust God to protect us and provide for us. I came to realize that it is impossible for me to please the Father without faith in His justice and generosity (see Hebrews 11:6).

It is easy to become offended every day by the people with whom we work. When this occurs, do we trust God for the gap between their actions and our expectations? In 1 John 4:10, the author shows that just as God lavished His love on us and took away our sins, so too we should do the same for others. Because God's goal is for us to be like Jesus, we must learn to forgive those who offend us as God forgives us of our sins.

POINT TO PONDER

LACK OF FORGIVENESS IS A SUBTLE TEMPTATION THAT CAN HAVE DEVASTATING RESULTS.

QUESTIONS TO CONSIDER

1. Are you in touch with the hurts you have experienced? Or have you succumbed to the toxins of anger and unforgiveness?

2. Do you have an unforgiving attitude toward work associates, particularly toward a supervisor or someone to whom you directly report?

3. How can you let go of that pain or lack of forgiveness and give it God? What steps can you take to make that happen at work and in other areas in your life?

It's Not About the Destination

Dianne Eckloff

FOUNDER AND PRESIDENT, BOSWELL BASSETT, INC.

28

Remain in me, and I will remain in you. No branch can
bear fruit by itself; it must remain in the vine. Neither can
you bear fruit unless you remain in me.

JOHN 15:4

Inspiration can come from a vision of what God has in store
for us down the road. But in the absence of such clarity, we
can find ourselves lacking diligence and daily motivation.
This is especially true when undertaking something new or
undefined. We can earnestly desire to do God's will, but
how do we proceed with passion and purpose when we
don't know where He is taking us?

When my business partner and I started our new company, we did so with the desire to devote our work to the
Lord. Yet while we sought His guidance on what we should

be doing, we have not received a clear picture from God on where we should be focusing our efforts. Because of this, I haven't had the confidence that we're really on God's chosen path for our business. As a result, I have been challenged daily with having the motivation and diligence to get our business going.

In pursuit of this clarity, I took some time away to fast and pray. During this time, the Lord showed me again and again that His Holy Spirit is powerfully in me. He does not make demands but waits for me to seek Him. When I walk with Him daily, I am in His will and He guides my every step.

Proverbs 3:6 states, "In all your ways acknowledge Him, and he will make your paths straight." As long as I follow this advice, I can know where I have peace and which steps I should take. For me, it is often the initial response I have to a situation that is the Holy Spirit. I am learning to trust it and know that it is a gift from God.

I know that I can often get off track when I think I know where I'm going and stop actively listening for God's voice. For instance, we once had a partner in our business who proved to be untrustworthy. Neither I nor the other partner had peace about him from the beginning, but we chose to ignore that feeling and follow his guidance and promises of success. Following his lead took us through two months of wild goose chases and dead-end paths.

Now, we are again seeking God's guidance. I ask the Holy Spirit to fill me each day and guide my actions and decisions, and He faithfully does. I still don't know where we will end up focusing our business, but I have the confidence and motivation that comes from knowing that we are on God's designated path and that He will guide our every step.

POINT TO PONDER

GOD IS MORE INTERESTED IN DIRECTING OUR
PATHS THAN IN PROVIDING A DESTINATION
FOR US TO REACH ON OUR OWN.

QUESTIONS TO CONSIDER

1. Do you have a clear picture of God's will for your life and your business?

2. Do you acknowledge God every step along the path? How do you think this affects those around you and even your own attitude at work?

3. Do you believe that God has a clear picture for your business or job? Will you ask Him to reveal that plan to you in all its clarity right now?

The MBA: Master of Baby Administration

Shelly Culpepper

Wife and Mother, The Culpepper Family
Former Marketing Manager, General Motors
and LifeScan, Inc.

29

*Do not work for food that spoils, but for food that endures
to eternal life, which the Son of Man will give you. On him God
the Father has placed his seal of approval.*

John 6:27

At the age of 32, I had earned an MBA, married the man of my dreams and was blessed with a job I truly loved. That year, I found out I was pregnant. Little did I know that my life would soon change forever.

When you're pregnant, it's easy to think that your world won't change much when you have a baby. That is, until you are brought face to face with a real person who is solely dependant on you for every little thing. Just months after our beautiful baby girl arrived, I was offered a promotion with the opportunity to go back to work part time. It was quite a tempting offer!

This threw me into a great deal of confusion. What would I do with my daughter, Kendall, if I went back to work? Could I be happy hiring a nanny or leaving her at day care? How would I know if she was getting enough sleep, enough food, enough love? On the other hand, what if I didn't go back to work? Would I be wasting my degree? What would my colleagues think if I didn't come back?

All of these questions led me to consider God's perspective. Which option would give Him the most glory— going back to work or staying at home?

Eventually, I realized that the product I was managing at work was just a product and certainly didn't have eternal significance when compared to a human life. As a wise friend shared with me, "Kendall is eternal." Furthermore, while I was replaceable as a marketing manager, I was the only one perfectly fit to be Kendall's mom.

My job now is to raise Kendall to know Jesus Christ so that she may one day choose to follow Him. My colleagues are the people we encounter during the day: the cashiers at the grocery store, our neighbors, the mailman, her music teacher, and, of course, other moms. How I serve them is a direct reflection of how Christ has changed me.

POINT TO PONDER

WORKING TO FURTHER GOD'S KINGDOM PRODUCES RESULTS
THAT LAST FAR BEYOND OUR TIME ON THIS EARTH.

QUESTIONS TO CONSIDER

1. Are you choosing to invest your time, energy and finances in things that are eternal or temporary?

2. Whether you are a working mom or a corporate executive, what are your real motives for getting up and working hard all day long?

3. Is the way you serve others a direct reflection of how Christ has changed your life?

LIVING AN INTEGRATED LIFE

KEITH FERRIN

FOUNDER AND PRESIDENT, TRUE SUCCESS COACHING, LLC

30

*Whatever you do, work at it with all your heart, as working
for the Lord, not for men, since you know that you will receive
an inheritance from the Lord as a reward.*

COLOSSIANS 3:23-24

It seems you can't pick up a business book or magazine these days without reading something about "work-life balance." Everything I read about a balanced life sounds really good. The problem is, I have a hard time actually doing it.

In fact, whenever I bring up the concept with someone, I can almost predict the eye roll followed by the heavy sigh. I have come to believe the reason for this is that God doesn't call us to a balanced life but rather an integrated life.

The primary metric for measuring a balanced life is time. If I spend this much time at work versus spending this much with my family, serving my community or worshiping at church, my life will be balanced.

Alternatively, the primary metric for measuring an integrated life is lordship. So, instead of determining how much time I am spending here or there, the real question becomes, Is Jesus Christ the Lord of every aspect of my life?

It is possible to live a balanced life yet not give Christ lordship over a certain area or areas of our life. Jesus wants to be Lord of everything—our work, family, friendships, leisure time and worship. The bottom line is that a balanced life can still be compartmentalized, but an integrated life cannot.

Paul begins the second half of his letter to the Ephesians with these words: "As a prisoner for the Lord, then, I urge you to live a life worthy of the calling you have received" (Ephesians 4:1). Here are just some of the areas of life he then goes on to discuss:

- Relationships
- Attitudes
- Reconciliation
- Our calling
- Service to the church
- Maturity
- Our minds

- Sexuality
- Honesty
- Work
- Our attitude toward money
- Our willingness to forgive others
- Our relationships with nonbelievers
- Wisdom
- Purity
- Marriage
- Our duties as parents
- Our relationships with bosses and employees
- Prayer
- Unity
- Our encouragement of one another in our calling

Now that's an integrated life!

Quite honestly, integration is harder than balance. But it's what we're called to do, and it leads to a sense of purpose and fulfillment that only comes from placing ourselves daily in the center of God's will. Integration requires examining our lives to see where we need to give Jesus His rightful place as Lord, discovering what we need to do in order to be obedient to His calling and executing those action steps, and conducting a regular evaluation that covers all areas of our lives.

Living an integrated life is a journey, not a task. There is no deadline. There is no chart or graph, just a constant prayer running through our minds: "Jesus, this day and every day, I give You Your rightful place as Lord of everything I am and do. When this day ends, may You be smiling. Amen."

POINT TO PONDER

GOD CALLS US TO LIVE AN INTEGRATED LIFE IN WHICH JESUS IS LORD OF EVERY PART.

QUESTIONS TO CONSIDER

1. What is one area of your life that you need to bring under the lordship of Jesus?

2. How do you see your life: an integrated journey or a balancing act? How does this affect your perspective of spirituality and God?

3. When today ends, will God be smiling on you?

LEADING LIKE JESUS

NANCY LAI

MBA CANDIDATE, THE WHARTON SCHOOL
MA CANDIDATE, THE LAUDER INSTITUTE

31

"Come, follow me," Jesus said, "and I will make you fishers of men."
At once they left their nets and followed him.

MARK 1:17-18

When I recently applied to competitive business schools, I was forced to think about what characteristics mark a good leader. In talking to seasoned business people and considering business literature, it became evident to me that the ability to successfully manage people is among a leader's top priorities.

How reassuring it is to know that Jesus Christ already modeled this type of leadership quality for us. Jesus' life was an example that no one person can do everything himself and that in order to have a great impact on people, we have to be willing to go out and find them, train them, invest in them and then empower them.

Jesus did this by gathering the 12 disciples that He selected to be His fishers of men and the builders of His church. He then equipped them with the necessary skills they would need to fulfill this purpose:

> When Jesus had called the Twelve together, he gave them power and authority to drive out all demons and to cure diseases (Luke 9:1).

Jesus took the disciples with Him throughout His three years of ministry on Earth, training and empowering them to be His representatives in this world. Sometimes He was frustrated at their lack of progress, but He persisted in developing them. Luke recounts Jesus' steps:

> He sent them out to preach the kingdom of God and to heal the sick. He told them: "Take nothing for the journey—no staff, no bag, no bread, no money, no extra tunic. Whatever house you enter, stay there until you leave that town" (vv. 3-4).

Jesus gave the disciples some detailed instructions, but ultimately He released the task into their hands. As a result, the disciples were very successful, "preaching the gospel and healing people everywhere" (v. 6).

Recently, this Scripture in Luke came alive to me when I met a South African female entrepreneur of a training and development business. She wanted to reach her country but had an "I need to do it all by myself" leadership style that was limiting her company's growth.

She left no time to develop new products or explore new markets. Concerned about quality, she taught most of the courses herself despite a willing staff who wished to be trusted with more.

How many of us overlook our own employees' needs, run ourselves ragged, and still do not achieve our company objectives? Are we heads of departments and companies because there is something inherently valuable in meeting quarterly targets? Or are we in these positions to work together in business as a means of accomplishing that goal?

At a recent event, I heard a former CFO from a Fortune 500 company speak about how his marriage problems stemmed from late night work during his company's formative years. When this executive forced himself to pack his briefcase and leave the office at 6 P.M. so that he could have dinner with his family, he soon found that he no longer needed to take work home.

This executive became better at managing his time and delegating responsibilities. He also discovered that those he managed were becoming much more satisfied with their greater job responsibilities. He saved his marriage, created happier employees, and his department continued to deliver.

To me, that's Jesus' leadership and life principles in practice.

POINT TO PONDER

JESUS WANTS US TO GET THE RIGHT PEOPLE ON BOARD IN OUR COMPANIES AND THEN INVEST IN THEM.

QUESTIONS TO CONSIDER

1. Whom do you admire as leaders? What particular traits do those individuals possess that you especially admire?

2. Do you want the same results as Jesus when He led? Do you trust Him for those results?

3. Are you trying to do everything yourself as a leader? What is wrong with this approach? How can you better trust and empower others to get things done?

LIVING THE KINGDOM LIFE

ERICK GOSS

VICE PRESIDENT OF MARKETING, MAGAZINES.COM

32

In a word, what I'm saying is, Grow up. You're kingdom subjects. Now live like it. Live out your God-created identity. Live generously and graciously toward others, the way God lives toward you.

MATTHEW 5:48, *THE MESSAGE*

I have often been struck with the challenges I've had as a Christian in the workplace and how difficult it has been for me to connect my day-to-day activities with what God is doing in the world. I used to think I was succeeding as a Christian if I had a vibrant devotional life, was contributing at church, and acting ethically at work. But all that changed a few years ago when I decided to take a sabbatical from serving as an elder at my church.

After leading the church through a very challenging crisis riddled by interpersonal conflict, I decided that I needed some time away. I had made significant sacrifices during the crisis and had seen my reputation attacked by a small but influential group in the church. While our church survived the controversy, I became deeply depressed.

One of the key questions I was asking myself was, *Is my personal relationship with God really worth the pain and sacrifice, or is there something bigger I'm missing?* While I found myself firmly rooted in Jesus Christ, I questioned whether I had missed His overall mission for my life.

As I searched the Scriptures for answers, I was struck by Jesus' emphasis on the kingdom of God and that for first-century Christians, Jesus' death and resurrection were more about God reestablishing His reign on Earth through Christ than on personal salvation. I realized that while my personal relationship with God is part of the story, it's not "the" story.

God's story is one of restoring His people and His world and making right all that is wrong. The question for me was whether I wanted to be a part of this story and whether I was willing to endure difficulties to see His reign and His gospel transform my church, my city and its institutions. I found that I had confused one of God's means (my relationship with Him) as an end unto itself and that I had missed the overall mission.

As I thought about living as if God's kingdom had come, I was struck the most by the implications in the marketplace. I recognized that living for the Kingdom meant living out Kingdom values wherever I was. It meant giving people a chance to experience the Kingdom through me.

I began wondering how I should manage my team and business in a manner that communicated God's character and kingdom. What would it mean for my peers to experience God's kingdom in their relationships with me? In all this, I recognized that living for Christ in the workplace was less about me and more about being a part of a greater movement to see His reign reestablished in my life, the marketplace, and the world.

POINT TO PONDER

LIVING AS A CHRISTIAN IN THE MARKETPLACE MEANS WORKING IN SUPPORT OF GOD'S EFFORTS TO REDEEM THE WORLD.

QUESTIONS TO CONSIDER

1. Are you more concerned about your relationship with God or with what God is doing in the world around you?

2. What does it mean for people to experience God's kingdom and character through you?

3. How does this impact how you manage your business and how you interact with others?

PRODIGAL ENTREPRENEUR

Ryan MacCarthy

Chief Entrepreneur, Nebo Group

33

This brother of yours was dead and is alive again; he was lost and is found.

LUKE 15:32

Throughout His life, Jesus built relationships. From the woman at the well to the thief on the cross, Jesus was attentive to relationships. He sought every opportunity to connect with people along the way.

Perhaps the most heartwarming parable that Jesus told was about a relationship between a father and his prodigal son. In this parable, told in Luke 15:11-32, the son decided to take his inheritance and leave his father for a life of self-fulfillment. He went out, squandered his wealth, and soon found himself left with nothing.

Hungry and alone, he decided to return to his father's house in the hopes his father would take him back as a servant. When the father saw his son coming back, he ran toward him and embraced him. "This son of mine was dead and is alive again," he proclaimed. "He was lost and now is found" (v. 24).

Now, I've never received an inheritance and run off to Las Vegas, but recently I've uncovered parallels to the parable in my own life. While bootstrapping for a start-up company, I borrowed significantly from my father. The company began growing and was soon in talks for acquisition, but we needed additional capital to move it forward.

A few months later, the acquisition went through, but some loose ends held us back from collecting the payment. As such, I wasn't able to repay my father. Yet the true severity of the situation didn't hit me until some time later when I heard from my father. "I knew there was a problem weeks ago," he said, "when you stopped calling me."

My heart sank as I realized that in the midst of my work—even toward a worthwhile goal—I had let my relationship with my father falter. More troubling was that I had lost focus on what was really important in the midst of an enormous blessing. This was especially painful to realize because it was my father's backing that enabled this blessing to occur in the first place. Like the parable of the prodigal son, my father was far more concerned about our relationship than about the money.

This experience taught me a great deal about how the Lord values our relationship with Him. Even though we may be pursuing worthy and worthwhile goals, what God really cares about is our personal connection with Him. He loves us for who we are, not for anything that we could hope to achieve in this life.

POINT TO PONDER

THE CULTIVATION OF HEALTHY RELATIONSHIPS IS THE FOUNDATION FOR GODLY BUSINESS PRACTICES.

REFLECTION QUESTIONS

1. How are you deepening your relationship with God through your work?

2. In what ways have you allowed relationships with others to falter because of your work?

3. How can you change this trend? What can you do to make sure that this does not happen again in the future?

What Does It Mean to Win?

Bruce Woolsey
Vice President, Avenue A/Razorfish

34

Now when he saw the crowds, he went up on a mountainside and sat down. His disciples came to him, and he began to teach them.

Matthew 5:1-2

In the highly competitive agency environment I inhabit most of the week, the thrill of victory can be intoxicating. Winning is pretty straightforward: You generate profit, get promoted and make more money.

My wife and I recently defined what winning means for our family. I was a bit overwhelmed at the challenge that definition represents on a daily, almost minute-by-minute basis. The yardstick of success in business is notched with riches, power and fame, but our family's faith demands the inverse: Generosity, service and humility are the measures of success. Winning in our home means turning the other cheek and loving others as we love ourselves.

I work in a great company where collaboration and mutual respect are defined as core values. It is also a performance-based culture, which I believe is critical to business success. But with performance comes an expectation of reward. It is here that challenges often arise: How often do I battle anger and frustration when I don't get the recognition I think I deserve? How often does my pride play a role in my attitude toward employees? How often do I view my income as rightful compensation to spend as I see fit?

If winning as a believer means growing in relationship with God and drawing others into relationship with Him, then we need to continually examine whether or not our actions reflect that goal. Failing to put our family first, treating subordinates as inferiors, and being political or divisive lead to failure. As Americans, we are conditioned to believe that recognition and reward follow performance, but our faith requires the pursuit of excellence without personal ambition.

The clearest definition of winning that Christ provides to us is found in His Sermon on the Mount. In this sermon, Jesus highlighted qualities such as meekness, peace making, purity of heart and thirsting after righteousness as those that indicate a winner in God's kingdom.

Perhaps like the rich young ruler in Mark 10:17-31, those of us in business face a bigger challenge than most:

to embrace the character of Christ in an environment where success is defined more simply and the yardstick of money, power and fame is visible to all. Yet as we go about our work, we need to remember that we are to fulfill God's purpose every minute of every day—and to remember that while we are in the world, we are not to be of it.

POINT TO PONDER

THE PURSUIT OF WORLDLY SUCCESS CAN OFTEN
LEAD TO FAILURE AS A BELIEVER.

QUESTIONS TO CONSIDER

1. How do you and your family define winning in life?

2. Jesus' definition of winning is often opposite of the definition used in the workplace. How can you make Christ's definition of winning a primary theme in your work life?

3. What do think of the phrase "our faith requires the pursuit of excellence without personal ambition"?

CALLED TO THE MARKETPLACE

AL ERISMAN

FORMER DIRECTOR, RESEARCH AND DEVELOPMENT,
THE BOEING COMPANY
DIRECTOR, CENTER FOR INTEGRITY IN BUSINESS,
SEATTLE PACIFIC UNIVERSITY

35

*For we are God's workmanship, created in Christ Jesus to do
good works, which God prepared in advance for us to do.*

EPHESIANS 2:10

A young Christian was working a job in logistics for a package delivery company. (Logistics is the planning and scheduling of the movement of goods so that products arrive on time where they are needed in an efficient manner.) He bemoaned the fact that his work was ordinary and wondered how he could find a job in full-time missions work that "counted" for God.

This young man obviously didn't know the biblical story of Joseph. God had personally come to Joseph's great-grandfather, Abraham, with the promise of making his family God's representative on Earth. The promise was repeated to his grandfather Isaac and to his father, Jacob. Joseph was in a prime position to be a leader in carrying out God's promise. But God had something else in mind for him.

Joseph was sold as a slave into Egypt, falsely imprisoned and forgotten. Then one day, someone he had helped in prison remembered him and suggested to the pharaoh that he was the very person who could help the pharaoh with a major problem. Not only did Joseph interpret the pharaoh's dream, but he also was commissioned to implement a plan to collect, store and distribute food to save the world in a time of famine. God cared about the distribution of goods then as he does now, and called Joseph to that work.

Joseph could have looked at his situation as being unworthy of his efforts, in light of the promise God had made to his family. But we see no evidence of this. Rather, we see a person who passionately and excellently pursued his job in logistics, serving God full time in a decidedly secular workplace.

This story of Joseph was an inspiration to me during the 32 years I worked at the Boeing Company. When I left the company to teach at a Christian university and publish *Ethix*, a friend said to me, "Now you are free to pursue the passion of your heart for the Lord."

My reply was, "I believe God called me to Boeing and, imperfect as I am, I was excited to serve Him there. Now I have a new opportunity to serve in another way. I believe I've always been in full-time Christian service."

POINT TO PONDER

NO MATTER WHO WRITES OUR PAYCHECK, WE MUST BE CAREFUL NOT TO TREAT OUR WORK AS ORDINARY.

QUESTIONS TO CONSIDER

1. In what way might God use your daily work for the benefit of His kingdom?

2. Do you need to remind yourself of this perspective from time to time?

3. Read through the story of Joseph in Genesis 37–50. How is the life of Joseph instructive in your own life?

Is Sin Crouching at Your Door?

Danny Kapic

INVESTMENT SALES, MARCUS AND MILLICHAP REAL ESTATE
INVESTMENT BROKERAGE COMPANY

36

I know, my God, that you test the heart and are pleased with integrity.
All these things have I given willingly and with honest intent.

1 CHRONICLES 29:17

Commercial real estate is a viciously competitive business. In my field of focus, the acquisition and disposition of investment properties, you only get paid when you close a deal. The concept of "team mentality" is not taught.

Temptation struck when the phone rang. It was a woman who owned a large apartment complex and who had been referred to me by a mutual acquaintance. She recently had a pricing evaluation done on her property and wanted a second opinion before deciding to sell. I knew that if I priced it aggressively, she would probably use me as her agent.

However, I immediately learned that another agent in my office had already completed the first pricing analysis. I had been sharing Christ with him during the past several months because he was in financial debt and looking for answers the world was not providing. I was now faced with a decision: I could undermine his efforts and take the listing myself or I could help him get the listing and get out of debt. My faith and integrity were being tested.

I thought about telling the woman I could get a higher price for the property, but the other agent had already priced it very aggressively, and his marketing proposal was excellent. I thought about co-listing the property with him, but he had put weeks of effort into getting the business. An honest evaluation would support his pricing conclusions. I also thought about informing the woman that the agent was younger and had less transactional experience, but in my heart I knew he would do an excellent job. Then I thought about Jesus Christ and what He would want me to do.

Fortunately, I decided to fix my heart on the things of God that day instead of taking immediate gratification. I honestly informed the woman that the agent was excellent, very capable, and that his pricing evaluation was accurate and aggressive. She decided to go with him.

Just this week, the building transaction closed, and he was able to pay off all his debts. He told me after it was all done, "Nobody else in this office would have done that for me. I know you really live out your faith." He also invited me to lunch. So now, I have another opportunity to share the hope that is in me and to offer him a salvation that provides eternal treasures.

We all have a debt of sin to pay, but fortunately the "paid in full" sign was placed on a cross a long time ago. Any time we choose heavenly treasures over earthly ones on behalf of another, the Kingdom advances.

POINT TO PONDER

IF WE DO NOT DO WHAT IS RIGHT, SIN IS CROUCHING AT OUR DOOR. IT DESIRES TO HAVE US, BUT WE MUST MASTER IT.

QUESTIONS TO CONSIDER

1. Are you building up earthly possessions but compromising your faith in the process?
2. When God tests your heart, is He pleased with your integrity? Why or why not?
3. Today, will you choose heavenly treasures over earthly ones on behalf of another? Will you choose to advance the Kingdom?

The Ultimate Headhunter

Brian Shepler

CFO, Ronald Blue and Company

37

"For I know the plans I have for you," declares the LORD, "plans to prosper you and not to harm you, plans to give you hope and a future."

JEREMIAH 29:11

If you were interviewing yourself for a job, would you hire you? I asked myself that question during a recent career transition and was paralyzed by the answer. Seven jobs in 10 years . . . What is wrong with this guy? Can't he hold down a job? Extracurricular activities look a little weak. What's with the ministry involvement? Where are the community board seats and Who's Who designations?

I'm not sure I would have lasted 15 minutes in an interview with me! At the same time, I found that I had become quite skilled over the years in the art of the job search. Multiple lines in the water, persistent follow-up, thorough interview preparation and mastery of the "30-minute good impression" had made me confident that I could land nearly any position for which I applied. So why was I doubting myself?

It seems that I had forgotten some important biblical truths and that God's plans were ultimately better for me than my plans. He was more concerned with where I was going than where I had been. Truth is, each of my previous assignments had provided me with unique experiences and allowed me to develop specific skills that perfectly prepared me for the corporate role in which I serve today. God clearly knew what He was doing!

As disciples of Christ, the command we have been given is quite simple: "Follow me" (Mark 10:21). There is a lot packed into those two words! In order to confidently follow Christ's lead, I find it helpful to remember His goodness, His faithfulness, His promise to complete that which He has begun (in me), and His gracious invitation to include me in *His* work.

If you are feeling down about your accomplishments or concerned about your future, remember that if you are following Christ's plan for your life, it doesn't matter what is or isn't on your résumé. You are exactly in the place where God wants you to be at precisely the right time. You can rely on the promises of God. After all, He is ultimately the best headhunter you could ever have!

POINT TO PONDER

GOD HAS A SPECIFIC JOB ASSIGNMENT AND CAREER
PATH ALREADY PLANNED FOR US.

QUESTIONS TO CONSIDER

1. Do you trust God to direct your career steps? Do you believe that He is ultimately the best headhunter you could ever have?

2. What do you think about the statement that God isn't as concerned about where you've been as much as He is about where you're going? How does that statement apply to your life?

3. Look back over your career so far. In what areas can you see God at work to guide you, protect you or teach you?

DOING THE
RIGHT THING

HUMAN RESOURCES, APPLIED BIOSYSTEMS

38

*Show me your ways, O Lord, teach me your paths; guide me in your truth and
teach me, for you are God my Savior, and my hope is in you all day long.*

PSALM 25:4-5

These days, it seems companies are eager to trumpet their
ethical principles. Respect and integrity are listed among
"Organizational Values." Honesty and open communication
are "Success Factors." Corporate brochures are peppered with
inspiring declarations of morality. It's hardly surprising, given
the recent moral failures in the marketplace.

In the business world, integrity is often elevated
because it enables companies to build trustworthy partnerships, gain consumer confidence, generate a positive culture, retain key talent and comply with rules and laws. But
because I am a Christian, I have a more compelling reason

to do the right thing than simply attaining material success, keeping my job and staying out of court.

According to the company's Core Beliefs, my employer pursues excellence because we believe in the power of science. Our customers are our top priority, we are accountable to our stockholders, and we value our people. In addition to these much-referenced and prominently displayed principles (all noble, to be sure), I am compelled to pursue excellence in my work because God is excellent, and my life's goal is to point others to Him. My aim must be to magnify Christ and to make Him look great. Fortunately for me, God gives me the strength and wisdom to choose wisely when I seek Him.

137

Today, I have a choice: I can offer an underperforming employee a transfer out of his current role and into another position, thereby avoiding a difficult conversation regarding his performance and the resulting conflict, or I can address the issue, sort through the consequences and walk with this colleague toward the goal of his development and greater productivity. My flesh pulls me along the path of least resistance—to encourage the transfer.

It's much more difficult for me to work with this employee to improve his performance (a process that will likely take months), but God has made it clear that this is the right course to take. It's what I must do to fulfill my job responsibilities with integrity and enable my company to live up to its commitment of valuing its people. It's also a way for Christ to be magnified in my work.

My ability to do my work, and to make right choices, is due to the unmerited favor of Christ. And I am so grateful, because it is painfully clear to me that my flesh lacks the ability to choose wisely.

POINT TO PONDER

GOD PROVIDES COUNSEL AND WISDOM
WHEN WE SEEK HIS GUIDANCE.

QUESTIONS TO CONSIDER

1. Do you depend on the Lord's guidance and counsel throughout your workday? Or do you rely on your own strengths and talents?

2. Do you allow God's priorities to shape your choices at work and at home?

3. Do your choices in the workplace point others to Him? Are you relying on His grace to help you make the right choices?

Commit Your Work to the Lord

Michael Yang

FOUNDER AND CEO, BECOME.COM

39

Commit to the LORD whatever you do, and your plans will succeed.

PROVERBS 16:3

In late 2003, after taking some time off from work, I decided to launch a new search engine venture called Become.com with my former business partner. Soon after we moved into a new office in early 2004, I invited the pastor of my church to come and have a service of prayer and blessing for our company at our new office.

The pastor and his wife brought a small gift for the opening of our office. It was a verse, Proverb 16:3, in both English and Korean, framed in a nice wooden frame. I love this verse. I hung it on the wall in my office directly in front of me and behind the computer monitor—a place where I can easily look up and see it every day. This verse has been a powerful word from God to me regarding both accountability and encouragement at work.

I feel called to be an entrepreneur in the marketplace. However, life as a founder and CEO of a Silicon Valley Internet start-up company can be both exhilarating and stressful.

The ups and downs are like a roller-coaster ride: When things go well, I am prone to become overly confident and prideful, but when things are down, I am prone to feel stressed out, insecure and discouraged. The Proverbs 16:3 verse that hangs on my wall is a great reminder to me during these times that God is in control.

Committing whatever I do to the Lord allows me to surrender both my work and my company to God each day. I no longer have to try to be in control and worry about all the fluctuations in my business. It also means that I am able to follow God's will for me at work, which is to love both the employees at the company and the people with whom I come into contact.

Commit to the Lord whatever you do,
and your plans will succeed.

This proverb is a good reminder to me that when we commit our work to the Lord, He will establish His plans in our business and in our life.

POINT TO PONDER

WE NEED TO COMMIT EVERYTHING THAT WE DO
IN OUR BUSINESSES TO THE LORD.

QUESTIONS TO CONSIDER

1. What are the areas in your line of work for which you need God's assurance and protection?

2. How can you make a bold commitment to the Lord in your business or job? What would be the outcome if you truly committed everything in your business to God?

3. How have you seen God establish His plans in your life? What plans do you want to see Him establish for you in the future?

How Do You Want to be Remembered?

Barry Landis
President, The Landis Agency

40

*A good name is more desirable than great riches; to be
esteemed is better than silver or gold.*
Proverbs 22:1

I was on a road trip to Atlanta recently when I noticed the writing on the back of a semi ahead of me that read, "What do you want on your Tombstone?"

Everyone else in the car understood it to be an advertisement for a pizza company, but I began thinking of it as a question that should cross the mind of every serious disciple of Christ. How do we want to be remembered when our work on Earth is done?

I've spent my career in the entertainment world, specifically in the music business, which, I have come to believe, is driven mostly by fear and ego. In this world, I want to be remembered as someone with character. I want my "yea to be yea" and my "nay to be nay" (see Matthew 5:37). I want to deal honestly with people, telling them the truth about our potential business together or why it's not going to happen. I want to deal with employees in a straightforward manner.

Character counts. In 1994, our company, Warner Alliance, had to take a stand on an issue with a gospel singer who had an affair with one of his background singers. We received both criticism and support for our decision to terminate the contract of the singer.

The local newspaper seemed amazed that a for-profit organization would have the resolve to take a moral stand, but my favorite response came from my former pastor, who said, "It is probably true that while the world continues to need preachments on issues such as this, it desperately needs examples."

"Character" has been defined as "moral or ethical strength." Right now in America, we desperately need examples of this type of character. All too often, we hear about another corporate scandal, another doping scandal in sports, another case of plagiarism by a journalist or student—even instances of ministers stealing sermons off of the Internet. "Everybody does it" should not be an excuse for the Christian.

God is constantly building our character. We don't get to choose our parents, but we do get to choose our character. We make decisions every day that shape our character,

143

determine our future course in life and, ultimately, establish what will be said about us when we are gone.

When Joseph was placed in bondage to the Egyptians, he was tested many times, yet he rose to the rank of the second most important person in all the country. His true character even allowed him to help the very brothers who had sold him into slavery.

In Victor Hugo's *Les Miserables*, the main character, Jean Valjean, thinks he has stolen silver from the bishop's home. However, when the police catch him and bring Valjean back to the scene of the crime, the bishop tells the police that he had given Valjean the silver. After the police leave, the bishop tells Valjean, "Now, you have been bought with a price. Use this money to become an honest man."

Paul tells us in 1 Corinthians 6:20, "Do you not know that your body is a temple of the Holy Spirit, who is in you, whom you have received from God? You are not your own; you were bought at a price. Therefore honor God with your body."

As Christians, we have been bought with a price. Since this is the case, how much more should we, who are called by His name, desire to use our bodies and minds in ways that demonstrate moral and ethical strength?

POINT TO PONDER

GIVE SO MUCH TIME AND ENERGY TO YOUR OWN IMPROVE-
MENT THAT YOU HAVE NO TIME TO CRITICIZE OTHERS.

QUESTIONS TO CONSIDER

145

1. What does the phrase "moral and ethical strength" mean in your life? How does this phrase make you think about your choices?

2. How can you make yourself an example of moral and ethical business in your everyday dealings with colleagues and other business people?

3. So . . . what do you want on your tombstone?

WHERE'S YOUR WORTH?

CINDY COMPERRY

ADVERTISING SALES PROJECT MANAGER, JOURNAL
COMMUNICATIONS

41

I have learned to be content whatever the circumstances . . .
I can do everything through him who gives me strength.

PHILIPPIANS 4:11,13

Asking people to give up a bit of their money has been my career. It sounds strange when I put it like that, but the truth is that I've been in both nonprofit fundraising and advertising sales, so asking for money is the name of my game.

With all that asking, I've been told "no" more times than I can count. "Our budget won't allow it this year." "Sorry, but we're cutting back on our advertising." "We've chosen another charity to support."

The goal in my current job is to close 30 percent of the sales I pitch. Ironically, that means that 70 percent of the people that I call on are expected to say no to my proposal.

Some say it loudly, some with regret, and some say it with an ego-charged drive to prove that they are in control.

I started wondering, *What if God only heard 30 percent of my prayers? What if I derived my worth from the 70 percent of people who tell me no along the way? What if Christ died on the cross for only 30 percent of my sins?* What a depressing life that would be! How would I even set the alarm clock in the morning to wake me for my next day's appointments?

Looking at the Bible, did Moses give up when the Israelites were inflicted with plagues as they wandered in the wilderness? No, he pressed on and depended on the Lord to get them to the Promised Land. Did Job renounce God when his whole life was taken from him? No. He had questions for God, but He never followed his wife's advice to just "curse God and die" (Job 2:9). These two individuals in the Bible put their lives in God's hands and pressed on despite the obstacles in their way.

In blending my Christian walk with my career, I've been praying through how to base my life not on the negative responses I receive but on the fact that I do close sales. The Lord does bless me, and He walks with me in each appointment. My purpose is to glorify God, regardless of whether or not I get a signed contract. My worth is huge in Christ's eyes.

I know that this is true because I was one of the many for whom Christ died a brutal death. That's where my purpose lies. That's where my worth lies. I'm a child of God, regardless of how much money I've brought into the company on any given day or week.

Whether you are in sales, leading a team of coworkers in a project or recruiting new employees, your worth is based on walking with Christ. An ability to close 30 percent, 50 percent or 100 percent of your calls is good, but not as great as knowing that Christ died for you, for me and even for the client who just said no.

Paul wrote in Philippians 3:8-9:

148

> I consider everything a loss compared to the surpassing greatness of knowing Christ Jesus my Lord, for whose sake I have lost all things. I consider them rubbish, that I may gain Christ and be found in him, not having a righteousness of my own that comes from the law, but that which is through faith in Christ—the righteousness that comes from God and is by faith.

I strive to keep these words in mind when I hear all those yeses and nos. I am appreciative when I close a sale, but I know that my worth does not come from the percentage of deals I close. My worth comes from something much greater. It comes from being a child of God.

POINT TO PONDER

OUR TRUE WORTH COMES FROM CHRIST
AND WHAT HE HAS DONE FOR US.

QUESTIONS TO CONSIDER

1. Do you approach each meeting as an employee or as a child of God?

2. Do you see your clients—even the ones who are hard to love—as fellow children of God?

3. Are you 100 percent committed to the One who is 100 percent committed to you?

THE ONLY NEWS WE NEED

BRIAN BATES

ASSIGNMENT MANAGER, WTVF-TV CBS AFFILIATE

42

Heaven and earth will pass away, but my words will never pass away.

MATTHEW 24:35

One of the fascinating aspects of working in television news is how quickly today's hot story can become yesterday's hype. The music and movie industries appear to have overnight sensations, but nothing like TV news. Any of us can become a newsmaker (whether or not we like it) if we happen to be at the right place (or the wrong place) at the right time.

For example, let's look at the story of Jason McElwain. Jason, who is autistic, was the 17-year-old senior manager of the basketball team at Greece Athena High School in Greece, New York.

In his team's final home game of the season, he entered the game with four minutes to go. It was his first and only appearance for the Athena High School varsity basketball team. Surprising the crowd, the 5-foot-6 manager hit six 3-point shots and a 2-pointer. When the buzzer sounded, Jason's team carried him off the court on their shoulders.

His triumph was captured on a student video that made the rounds of all the major television networks, and it made Jason an instant celebrity. His was the interview every news outlet *had* to have.

Today, few people remember the name Jason McElwain or his inspiring story. Most newsmakers' fame lasts only as long as the next big story. Maybe it's a day, a week, or even a month, but pretty soon we've moved on to something else.

That is what's so amazing about the good news of Jesus Christ. It's been reported for more than 2,000 years! The gospel spread like wildfire all over the world without the help of the Internet or CNN Headline News. Why? Because its message is the only news people really need.

Osama Bin Laden, Lance Armstrong, Hurricane Katrina—these are some recent newsmakers that we won't soon forget. But eventually, even these names will only be remembered in our history books.

The news of Jesus Christ, however, will be broadcast all over the globe for all eternity. As He said in Matthew 24:35, "Heaven and earth will pass away, but my words will never pass away."

We should all be news anchors, reporters and writers of the message of Jesus. His words should be the lead story in all of our lives.

POINT TO PONDER

THE GOOD NEWS OF JESUS CHRIST
REQUIRES US ALL TO BE NEWSCASTERS.

QUESTIONS TO CONSIDER

1. What's making the headlines in your life? Your career? Your family? Is it Jesus Christ?

2. How can you be a newscaster for God at work, especially when you can talk to the biggest celebrity in the universe? What does this mean for you?

3. How can your lifestyle broadcast volumes to those around you without you even saying a word?

EXPECT TRIALS

CHERYL BACHELDER

FORMER PRESIDENT, KFC RESTAURANTS
CONSULTANT TO THE WOMEN'S FOODSERVICE FORUM

43

Consider it pure joy, my brothers, whenever you face trials
of many kinds, because you know that the testing of
your faith develops perseverance.

JAMES 1:2-3

I am an optimist. My favorite childhood story was *The Little Engine That Could,* the story of the train that climbed the mountain saying, "I think I can, I think I can . . ."

This mantra characterized my life, and certainly my business career. I wanted to work on the rusty old brands that had lost relevance to their customers. I wanted to inherit a poorly performing team and turn it around. I wanted to be given the impossible goal that had stymied prior leaders. Bring it on.

Then came the trials. While serving as the leader of a large chain restaurant corporation, God saw fit to test me. First, I was diagnosed with cancer and had to undergo surgery and radiation treatments. Then, barely nine months later, I experienced a second health crisis that required surgery and a two-month medical leave.

Simultaneously, the business took a sharp turn south, and nothing that our team put in the marketplace arrested the trend. It was like being in the ring facing a world-class boxer with no training on how to avoid the opponent. I took the hits hard, first on the left cheek, then on the right, then in the gut. I was stunned. I couldn't steady myself. I thought I would go careening into the ropes.

What was wrong with my perspective? Simply this: I did not expect the trials. I thought I was immune to them. My optimism—a strength in many settings—was now my greatest weakness.

The Bible says unequivocally that we will face trials of many kinds. These trials are the intentional plan of God for the refinement of our faith. Trials are God's way of enrolling us in His character-building program.

Today, I am deeply grateful for these trials in my life. I have been refined by fire—fire that humbled me and caused me to once again surrender everything to my Lord and Savior, Jesus Christ. This was God's perfect plan to make me a better witness for Him in the world.

To God be the glory.

POINT TO PONDER

TRIALS ARE GOD'S PLAN TO BUILD OUR CHARACTER
AND REFINE OUR FAITH.

QUESTIONS TO CONSIDER

1. How are you responding to your trials at work and at home? Are you angry, frustrated or disappointed?

2. Can you see how God's character might be revealed in the way you respond to these difficulties?

3. Have you surrendered these trials to the saving grace of your Savior, Jesus Christ?

Resting in God's Arms

Wes Bolsen

Senior Associate, McKinsey and Company

44

Come to me, all you who are weary and burdened, and I will give you rest. Take my yoke upon you and learn from me, for I am gentle and humble in heart, and you will find rest for your souls.

Matthew 11:28

I am tired of getting on planes and feeling the need to continue working during the flight. I'd rather spend time talking to other passengers and showing love to them. The business world is full of people like me, working lots of hours because it is our "job." There are a lot of ways to fool ourselves into thinking that we are doing something noble by working 60 to 70 hours per week. We even try to fool our Christian friends by saying we are working as if we are doing it for the Lord.

I didn't want to address the topic of resting. As a consultant, I get on a lot of planes, work late nights and feel as if I make a difference in the business world. However, one weekend when I was invited to a contemplative retreat, it struck me that I have a hard time simply resting. Some of my friends on the retreat wrestled with God and contemplated Scripture. But what I felt God was saying to me was, "Rest in my arms."

The first step in receiving this rest for my soul was to come to Christ. The word that I kept hearing was, *Stop! Stop doing all of the things that are keeping you so busy and distracted. Stop the work you do for the world. I (Christ) don't want to add more to your list of obligations to be a Christian. I simply want you to rest in My presence and know you are loved.* So I put down my Bible, let peace come over me, and lay down on a park bench and slept.

157

During that weekend, I was called to a Scripture in Matthew 11:28, in which Jesus says, "Come to me, all you who are weary and burdened, and I will give you rest. Take my yoke upon you [be tied to Christ] . . . and you will find rest for your souls. For my yoke is easy and my burden is light."

A second passage of Scripture that really spelled this out for me was Psalm 23:1: "The Lord is my shepherd . . . He makes me lie down in green pastures, he leads me beside quiet waters, He restores my soul." That is pretty awesome to think about: lying out in a sunny field with a stream going by while Jesus watches out for me, ready to fight off wolves if they come. He wants to be my friend. He wants to love and protect me, but He also wants me to rest.

Why is it that I get so busy? Is it really working for the Lord? What does it mean to truly rest in His arms? I am not sure, but what I can say without a doubt is that God called me on that day to stop and rest in His arms. The challenge for me is to shut out all the noise and simply be in His presence. What does that look like for you?

POINT TO PONDER

REST IS A SPIRITUAL DISCIPLINE.

QUESTIONS TO CONSIDER

1. What does it truly mean to stop and do nothing? What are you trying to prove if you choose to work 60 to 70 hours per week?

2. How can you take the time to stop and just rest in God's arms today or this week?

3. Do you ever feel weak or burdened? Open yourself to the idea of resting this week—not while watching TV or resting on a business flight, but truly resting!

WALKING IN HUMILITY

MONICA PATRICK

PROCUREMENT ANALYST, CONOCOPHILLIPS COMPANY

45

Do nothing out of selfish ambition or vain conceit, but in
humility consider others better than yourselves.

PHILIPPIANS 2:3

I spent time praying for humility one recent morning before work. I asked God to help me be more gracious to people on the road during rush hour and also to be humble when I was asked to perform a task at work that I deemed beneath my position.

It was a quiet time of repentance and asking the Father to be glorified in my life that I might dwell with Him "in the high and holy place" (Isaiah 57:15). I finished up my prayers and felt calm, collected and serene. Then I arrived at work . . .

I'm always amazed when God actually takes me at my word and asks that I be accountable to those things I've discussed with Him in prayer. I logged on to my computer, and the first e-mail that I read, quite honestly, made me fume. So, I reacted.

I'm certain the world would not have seen anything wrong with my response. The e-mail I received was inappropriate. I did not rant and rave or act unprofessionally. However, the Father reminded me of the humility we had discussed earlier and that I, as a follower of Christ, have been called to a different standard.

In today's marketplace, we each have a drive to be successful, advance our careers, make a name for ourselves and not allow others to push us around. It is a selfish ambition, in which we seldom esteem others better than ourselves.

Rarely are we applauded for approaching life with a lowliness of mind. But God highly reveres humility. His Word says He "opposes the proud, but gives grace to the humble" (James 4:6).

Grace to the humble . . .

Grace as I humbly submit to those God has placed in authority over me in my job . . . grace as I humbly surrender those things I think I deserve . . . grace as I humbly complete the task at hand, no matter how menial I believe it to be.

God, help me to walk in humility so that You will continue to pour out Your grace on my life!

POINT TO PONDER

LET NOTHING BE DONE THROUGH
SELFISH AMBITION OR CONCEIT.

QUESTIONS TO CONSIDER

1. How would your attitude at work change if you were to actively pursue the mind of Christ?

2. Why do you think God gives grace to the humble and lifts up the meek? How do you think He will lift you up if you seek these qualities?

3. Can you think of one recurring instance at your place of work that might be changed if you were to act—or react— with grace?

FRUITS OF OUR LABOR

MANKA JOHNSON

PARTNER, ONEACCORD

46

But the fruit of the Spirit is love, joy, peace, patience,
kindness, goodness, faithfulness, gentleness and self-control.
Against such things there is no law.

GALATIANS 5:22-23

I spent this afternoon at the farmer's market. As I wandered through the stalls, I could smell peaches long before I reached the stall where they were being sold. Once I tasted one, I couldn't resist the urge to buy a few.

The peaches now sit on my kitchen counter. As I glance at them, I reflect on John 15:4: "Remain in me, and I will remain in you. No branch can bear fruit by itself; it must remain in the vine. Neither can you bear fruit unless you remain in me." And I wonder, *Apart from memories of an enjoyable afternoon, what will remain after the last peach is eaten?*

I believe that the fruit of the Spirit listed in Galatians 5:22-23 describes Christ. Whenever I attempt to describe

Christ to someone, I inevitably use the characteristics contained in that verse: loving, joyful, peaceful, patient, kind, good, faithful, gentle, self-controlled. I believe that as I follow Him, I'm continually growing in my capacity for having these same characteristics.

Scripture describes these gifts as fruit. I think one reason for this is to make a distinction about their origin. These characteristics grow; they are not self-assembled. I don't have a formula for joy. I haven't figured out a design specification for peacefulness. On the other hand, I know that when I experience joy, it results in thoughts, words and actions that others may recognize as joyful.

163

It's interesting to me that John 15 places the topic of fruitfulness within the context of love. For me, it reinforces the belief that my relationship with Christ is the source of any fruitfulness I have. In other words, many of my thoughts, words and actions ultimately result from how I imagine Christ—what I actually believe about Him and what I believe about myself as a result. If my image of Christ aligns with the descriptors used in Galatians, my hope is that the characteristics I display will resemble those descriptors more and more.

As a consultant, I've spent a lot of time thinking about why clients choose to do business with my company. Ultimately, something about the offering or solution that we present attracts them. But once a consulting relationship begins, the results often extend farther than anyone imagined. Long after a consulting relationship ends, something remains—a seed—that may eventually produce positive secondary effects.

Accepting Scripture's teaching about fruitfulness leads me to believe that some of these results are spiritual in nature.

POINT TO PONDER

IF WE ARE CONSCIOUS ABOUT OUR RELATIONSHIP WITH CHRIST, OUR ACTIONS WILL EXHIBIT WHAT WE BELIEVE ABOUT HIM TO OTHERS.

QUESTIONS TO CONSIDER

1. Do you imagine Christ as having the gifts of the Spirit as described in Galatians 5:22-23?

2. What are the ways the fruit of the Spirit impacts your demeanor, attitude, communication style, work style, output and relationships at work?

3. How can you remain conscious of your relationship with Christ in the workplace?

You Have to Build It to Know It Floats

Tom Horvath

CHAIRMAN, BERKELEY COURT ADVISERS

47

But I will establish my covenant with you, and you will enter the ark—
you and your sons and your wife and your sons' wives with you.

GENESIS 6:18

As I approach two successful decades of being in the corporate world, I am faced with a decision. Should I stay or should I go? These days, it is a decision that most people will face several times during their career.

In my personal situation, I feel led to leave what I have known—working for a company—and launch my own firm. I have prayed for doors to open, and they have opened. I have prayed for doors to close, and they have closed. Short of finding a letter from God dropped down from heaven (I'm still looking for it!), I'm typing my resignation letter this weekend.

I am thankful to have peace in this leap of faith that I am taking. My decision is not based on wanting more—more money, more power, more success—but on wanting more of God. I want to know Him more, trust Him more, love Him more and experience Him more in a powerful way.

I thought I was doing pretty well with all of this (and feeling pretty spiritual about it, too), but then reality hit. Yesterday, I was updating a friend about my impending decisions when my usually confident voice began to quiver and my dry eyes filled with tears.

I told my friend, "You know, I trust God completely with my life, but I don't trust Him with my family. Personally, I will walk wherever He leads, but taking my family there is another matter. I still feel that I need to have everything figured out so that I can take care of them and protect them."

When God spoke to Noah, Noah's family was part of the message. As I read through the account, I discovered something interesting: In Genesis 6:18, God promised that He would establish a covenant with Noah, but it wasn't until Genesis 9:9—after Noah's obedience to build an ark, gather his family in the wooden boat, and spend 40 days and nights in the smelly thing—that God revealed the covenant to Noah and his family.

Noah heard, Noah obeyed, and God blessed him. So who am I to want the order reversed?

Point to Ponder

What is it about God's faithfulness that we don't think is good enough for us?

Questions to Consider

1. In what areas of your life are you trying to figure out God's promises before figuring out how to be obedient?

2. Is your walk of faith a solo journey, or do you let people walk with you?

3. How do you see God's faithfulness in your life today? Are you striving to be obedient to His will in all things?

MAKING THE MOST OF IT

ELISABETH WADSWORTH

CONSULTANT, HEALTHCARE INDUSTRY

48

Be very careful, then, how you live—not as unwise but as wise, making the most of every opportunity, because the days are evil.

EPHESIANS 5:15-16

Make the most of every opportunity! This phrase sounds like a sales manager talking to his or her ambitious team, doesn't it? Yet those who are focused on closing the deal know that discretion is always needed to decide where to focus and on whom to focus.

This principle is echoed in Scripture. In Ephesians 5:15, Paul says that we must live wisely. In business culture, we are often required to present ourselves as competent and ambitious in order to compete effectively. We are trained to look at new relationships as opportunities for new sales or new partnerships and to envision challenges as opportunities for growth. God will work with, through and in spite of these frameworks, but only if we allow Him to use us.

The Lord wants to use not only our time but also our expertise, our finances and even our position within an organization. This requires us to come before the Lord in prayer, asking for His priorities and the ability to see the opportunities that He presents to us throughout our day. The trick is not in trying to demonstrate Christ to more people in our day, but in learning to see our days as God sees them—as opportunities to lay down our own ambitions and allow God to prioritize our actions.

Recently, I failed an exam that was critical to my career development. I would have preferred to deal quietly with the consequences and to prepare to retake the exam at a later date. But God had other plans. He asked me to reach out to my teammates and ask for their help. I thought, *What could ruin my reputation more quickly than publicly highlighting my weaknesses to those who will have an impact on the future of my career?*

But God's calculus is different from ours. What I saw as a failure, He saw as an opportunity to teach others. I had to decide where my ambition lay: in trying to protect my reputation or in paving the way for God's works to be evident. Obeying God not only demonstrated His faithfulness in caring for my wellbeing but also enabled four professionals to see business modeled in an attention-getting way. "Make the most of every opportunity."

When opportunities came your way this past week, did you see them? You have heard the message before that God wants to use you to minister to others through your actions and words. But be on the lookout! God wants to use you *today* to exemplify His way of how business should be conducted!

Point to Ponder

To truly make the most of every opportunity for God, we must try to see every day as God sees it.

Questions to Consider

1. Can you be ambitious and demonstrate the good news at the same time? Are the two ever in conflict?

2. How can you see today—and every other day—the way God sees it?

3. What are some opportunities facing you that God might want to use to further His kingdom? Have you prayed about these opportunities?

LORD, SAVE ME!

GENE SHACKELFORD

FORMER PLANT MANAGER, UNION CARBIDE

49

Commit your way to the LORD; trust in him and he . . .
will make your righteousness shine like the dawn, the justice
of your cause like the noonday sun.

PSALM 37:5-6

"So, this is what a nervous breakdown is like!" I almost screamed out as I lay awake late one night.

I was experiencing the shakes—something I had never experienced before—and I was terrified. I had taken a new job as plant manager of a large chemical plant that was having major organizational problems. I had been in the job about a month and things were *not* going well.

There were serious conflicts between the members of the plant management team, and, as a result, serious labor union problems were developing. This was all being heated up by constant warnings from headquarters: "This mess better get straightened out soon!" Why did I take this job anyway?

The impact of all this came down on me all at once that night in bed. Out of desperation, I got up and, without waking my wife, started reading the psalms as I had never read them before. "Lord, help me!" I cried out, like Peter did as he was sinking into the water beside Jesus.

I soon came across Psalm 37:5, which says, "Commit your way to the Lord; trust in Him and he will do this." I had read that verse many times before, but this time it had a whole new meaning. I committed to do just that. I went back to bed and immediately went to sleep. The next morning, I shared all this with my wife, and she joined me in praying about the situation.

The problems did not go away immediately, but my attitude about them changed instantly. It was amazing how even when I had no clue which way to go, the Lord directed organizational changes in the right direction. I had to make some very painful personnel decisions. In many cases, I felt very much alone. But I continued to read the psalms, and my wife and I continued to pray together for guidance.

The entire situation improved over time, but more important for me, my walk with the Lord grew stronger each day as I committed my way to Him and understood what it meant to seek His guidance in all things—even corporate organizational issues.

POINT TO PONDER

THE LORD WANTS US TO COMMIT EVERY DECISION TO HIM.

QUESTIONS TO CONSIDER

173

1. How do you trust God for guidance in the midst of an organizational or personal crisis?

2. What does this kind of trust and reliance on God do to change your relationship with Him?

3. Do you ever feel alone in making hard decisions? How does this reading change your perspective on that issue?

ENCOURAGEMENT IN THE WORKPLACE

CAROLYN NORTON

PROGRAM COORDINATOR, COCA-COLA SCHOLARS FOUNDATION

50

Let us consider how we may spur one another on toward
love and good deeds . . . let us encourage one another—and all the
more as you see the Day approaching.

HEBREWS 10:24-25

Whether you are a parent, teacher, aunt or uncle, you know that children thrive on praise. For six years after college, I taught second-graders. During that season of life, I was able to see firsthand how positive discipline encouraged my students to do better. I discovered that negative comments only hindered their ability to learn.

Now that I'm in the corporate world, I realize more and more that even as adults we need positive feedback and encouragement in our jobs. Unfortunately, it doesn't happen that often. For instance, when I hear my boss say, "I think you did a great job on this and here are some suggestions I have to improve it," I am encouraged much more than if he said, "That was terrible and I think you need to change it to my way."

We all need constructive criticism! But the way that criticism is presented can mean the difference between an employee who feels motivated to want to work harder and an employee who is left feeling broken down and discouraged. As Christians, God calls us to encourage and spur each other on in our daily lives.

The word "encourage" means to inspire with confidence, to give hope or to contribute to someone's progress or growth. Encouraging goes far beyond the mere giving of gifts or compliments to others and making them feel good. It is also the way that we unselfishly spend time with others, listening to them, giving them helpful advice or offering them a passage from Scripture. Encouraging might mean helping someone to seek another career, lose weight, get out of a bad relationship, make an important financial decision, or even to seek wise counsel.

You may find that you would often rather pray for someone than talk to him or her. At times encouraging others will seem awkward and difficult to do. If encouraging others is hard for you, challenge yourself to step out of your comfort zone. Just like the word itself, to "encourage" someone often takes "courage." Encouraging another person isn't always pleasant. Sometimes, it can even be considered tough love.

Even though tests have shown that encouragement is a spiritual gift of mine, it is still hard for me! I tend to shy away from the more difficult discussions that I know I need to have with someone. There is never a comfortable time to encourage or have that awkward talk. Yet God calls us to do it daily. You may consider asking God to show you *how* to encourage, rather than *when* to encourage.

Regardless of the way we are compelled to encourage, consider what Colossians 3:15-17 tells us:

> Let the peace of Christ rule in your hearts, since as members of one body you were called to peace. And be thankful. Let the word of Christ dwell in you richly as you teach and admonish one another with all wisdom, and as you sing psalms, hymns and spiritual songs with gratitude in your hearts to God. Whatever you do, whether in word or deed, do it all in the name of the Lord Jesus, giving thanks to God the Father through him.

So ask yourself, *Who is it in my life that needs to be encouraged?* It could be a matter of spiritual life or death for someone close to you.

POINT TO PONDER

TO ENCOURAGE SOMEONE AND INSPIRE HIM OR HER
WITH CONFIDENCE REQUIRES COURAGE ON OUR PART.

QUESTIONS TO CONSIDER

177

1. Who in your life needs encouraging?

2. How can you challenge yourself to step out of your comfort zone to encourage someone?

3. When do you find it difficult to encourage others? Why do you think that is the case?

MANAGING YOUR TALENTS

MARK McCLAIN

CEO, SAILPOINT TECHNOLOGIES

Because of the service by which you have proved yourselves,
men will praise God for the obedience that accompanies
your confession of the gospel of Christ.

2 CORINTHIANS 9:13

One of the challenges I face as I seek to apply biblical truth to my life is ensuring that I properly understand the meaning of Jesus' parables.

These stories, which Jesus told using real-life examples in a first-century Jewish culture, are often somewhat foreign to me, living in twenty-first-century America. (I don't know about you, but I've never actually seen a mustard seed or yeast!)

However, one of the easiest parables for me to apply, especially in the modern-day world of work, is the familiar parable of the talents found in Matthew 25 and Luke 19. The basic premise of the story is that a master (e.g., CEO) provides different amounts of money (resources) to his servants (managers) and then waits to see what they do with it.

Two of the three managers put the money to work and double it for the CEO. The third manager, however, decides to bury it and return it to his boss with no increase. Needless to say, the CEO finds this totally unacceptable and fires him. He then gives that manager's resources to the highest-performing manager.

Three things have always struck me about this story. First, the boss provides almost no concrete direction to the managers. He simply provides them with resources and then lets them use their abilities and talents to provide the best results they can.

Second, he doesn't provide each manager with the same amount, which seems to imply that he already suspects that different members of his team have different abilities.

Third, although the CEO gives the second manager less, he provides the same level of commendation to him as he does to the first manager, because both of them doubled his investment.

It strikes me that we can learn a great deal about effective management from this story. In fact, the story provides us with great insight into both the management of our own

God-given resources and the management of the resources He provides to us in business, especially human resources.

God doesn't micromanage us, and He doesn't want us to micromanage others. He expects us to honestly assess ourselves and those under our direction to maximize the Kingdom impact of what we have been given.

Far too often as leaders, we don't allow people to use their creativity and initiative to solve problems. We need to let people show us what they can do with what we entrust to them, just as God expects that of us.

God also shows us through this story that we shouldn't show favoritism when showering praise. We need to remember the same rule we were taught as children playing sports or learning an instrument: Do your best.

Of course, we have to recognize those who are more gifted and generally give them more responsibility. But we should never forget the importance of praising each and every person who does the absolute best with what he or she has been given.

Nothing is more motivating to a worker than to hear, "Well done!" God has entrusted each of us with so much. May we all strive to consistently deliver a great return on His investment in us.

POINT TO PONDER

GOD PROVIDES EACH OF US WITH DIFFERENT ABILITIES BUT
EXPECTS US TO MAKE THE MOST OF WHAT WE'VE BEEN GIVEN.

QUESTIONS TO CONSIDER

181

1. Are you a good manager of the resources, both personal
   and professional, that God has given to you?

2. How are you making the most of the gifts, abilities and
   resources that God has given to you?

3. How are you praising others at work as they learn to manage their own talents?

God's Creativity in Job Placement

Amy Fritz

PRINCIPAL, STRATEGIC DIALOGUES

52

It was he who gave some to be apostles, some to be prophets, some to be evangelists, and some to be pastors and teachers, to prepare God's people for works of service, so that the body of Christ may be built up.

EPHESIANS 4:11-12

"Well, I guess the business world needs caring and compassionate people, too," my college faculty advisor sighed after presenting me with a Human Development Outstanding Achievement Award at graduation. Under her supervision, I completed a number of social services internships in preparation for a career in social work.

However, during the summer before my senior year, I had taken a temporary job at a Silicon Valley technology company. Now, at graduation, I decided to take a brief detour into business. What I thought would be a couple of years ended up stretching into 25 years, so far.

Many times, I have questioned that decision and whether I am on the career path God had planned for me. I often long for a career such as social work where my work would be clearly focused on helping people.

During these times of questioning, the words of my secular faculty advisor often come back to me. She was right—the business world needs caring and compassionate people. God knows this and has placed me in business to be a "social worker," although that is not the title on my business card.

Through a variety of roles I have held in finance and marketing management, I have had the opportunity to interact with people who are in the prime of their life and very successful by worldly standards. Many of these people live comfortably and feel little need for God. When these people face hardships, they do not know where to turn. It is important that compassionate and caring workplace believers are there to show them the way.

On a broader level, I have used my position in business to lobby for stakeholders who may not have a voice in the executive suite. I have had the opportunity to help reshape strategies, communications and products so that they honor customers, employees and the community. At the same time, the results often improved the company's return.

Infinitely creative, God is not limited by a list of known job titles and typical career progression plans. For many of us, His plan will parallel the logical training and progression for a specific career. But we shouldn't limit ourselves—or God—to career paths defined by worldly tradition. He may have other plans for us!

POINT TO PONDER

GOD IS INFINITELY CREATIVE AND HAS A UNIQUE CAREER PATH DESIGNED FOR US.

QUESTIONS TO CONSIDER

1. Where is God, the Creator, calling you to practice your vocation? Have you yielded to His call?

2. In what ways do you see your career path as unique and designed by God?

3. Have you ever limited yourself in your vocation by telling yourself you can't do something? Have you ever asked God to expand your thinking as to your career path and career choices?

THE RIGHT KIND OF AMBITION

PRESIDENT AND CEO, MADE FOR SUCCESS

53

*Make it your ambition to lead a quiet life, to mind your own business
and to work with your hands, just as we told you.*

1 THESSALONIANS 4:11

Can Christians be ambitious? That question haunts many
Christian business people who want to be devoted to Christ
but who also feel a compelling drive to succeed in the marketplace. We want to succeed in business, but we feel that
we should not long for the things of this world.

The question I ask myself is this: Is God ambitious? The
answer is unequivocally yes. After all, what ambitious plans
could top the goal of creating a hundred million galaxies?
God's plan to become a man and single-handedly save
mankind from its fallen state is the essence of compassionate ambition. God, by His very nature, is ambitious.

So, where does that leave us? We were created in the image of God to reflect the nature of God. That means that we as Christians should be ambitious, for when we are ambitious, it shows the world the very nature of God. As a caveat, at the same time we are called to reflect the character of God.

This brings us to the kind of ambition that we should *not* demonstrate—selfish ambition. Paul writes, "The acts of the sinful nature are obvious: sexual immorality, impurity and debauchery . . . selfish ambition, dissensions, factions" (Galatians 5:20; see also Philippians 1:17; 2:3). James states, "Where you have envy and selfish ambition, there you find disorder and every evil practice" (3:16).

Never does the Bible tell us to not be ambitious, but it does tell us five times that selfish ambition is not of God. We demonstrate the character of God in our ambition when we avoid selfish ambition and instead demonstrate selfless ambition. The key is to always be aware of the state of our heart.

Are we ambitious because God has placed a desire in our heart to achieve a dream that glorifies Him? Then we should pursue it with all our hearts! But if we find that there are selfish motives in our ambition, we need to take the time to pray and ask God to show us His ambitious plans for our lives. It is our job to wait on God, hear His voice and pursue His ambitious plan.

POINT TO PONDER

SELFLESS AMBITION TRIUMPHS OVER
UNHEALTHY AMBITION EVERY TIME.

QUESTIONS TO CONSIDER

187

1. Are your plans selfish or selfless? Does the very fact that you have made plans necessarily mean that they will be carried out or completed?

2. Are you pursuing a dream or desire that God has placed in your heart that will ultimately glorify Him? How can you surrender your own ambitions and join in God's plan?

3. Are you demonstrating the character of God in your ambitions? What might be the end result of living a life of selfless ambition?

FINDING GOD IN
THE MOUNTAINS

ED DIFFENDAL

DIRECTOR, BUSINESS DEVELOPMENT,
SYMANTEC SOFTWARE

54

After six days Jesus took with him Peter, James and John the brother of
James, and led them up a high mountain by themselves.

MATTHEW 17:1

Have you ever wondered what Christ did when He wasn't working? During the period of His life that we know about from the
Gospels, Christ's life was His ministry: teaching, preaching,
healing, feeding. But a close examination of the Gospels reveals
that Christ frequently took time alone to recharge.

Jesus often got away from the crowds, His disciples and
other followers. Almost always, He went to the mountains.
Some of the most profound parts of Christ's ministry occurred in or immediately after He retired to the high places:
the Sermon on the Mount, the transfiguration, His betrayal,
His crucifixion.

Our work, whatever it is, creates layers of concern that come between us and God. The "mountains"—those places we get away to spend time alone with God—allow the Lord to peel away those layers to get to the core of who we are. That process is both essential to our life with God and essential to us being faithful people of God when we go back to work.

I recently came back from climbing to the top of the world. Getting to the top of Mount Everest is a grueling process. I endured bitter cold, oxygen deprivation, dangerous crevasses and long, long days of working hard at high altitude. Of course, while I found that this process had a dramatic effect on my body, it also had a dramatic effect on my soul. Petty disagreements with colleagues, bad presentations, figuring out which e-mails were or weren't replied to, all slowly stopped dominating my mind. I found that I was free to listen to what God had to teach me about my life.

The teachings were simple and rich: huge soaring mountains . . . God is God; the provision of a weather window or a secure axe placement . . . we should trust God; the realized triumph of the summit . . . God loves us; the camaraderie and teamwork of our partners . . . we should love others the way God loves us.

What is your Everest? The absolute magnitude of the experience doesn't matter. What does matter is how much what you are doing pushes you to rely on God. Go climb

189

Half Dome. Hike Mount Washington. Run a triathlon. Walk that one extra loop in the park or on the beach. Then simply listen. Psalm 46:10 says it best: "Be still, and know that I am God."

POINT TO PONDER

WE NEED TO SPEND TIME OUTSIDE OF WORK IN A PLACE THAT PEELS AWAY THE LAYERS SO THAT GOD CAN SPEAK TO US.

QUESTIONS TO CONSIDER

1. Think about what it means when God says, "Be still, and know that I am God." Is there a place where you go that allows you to do this?

2. If climbing an actual mountain is not an option for you, where can you go and what can you do to come to a place of rest and reliance on God?

3. How are you patterning your life after Christ with regard to getting away to gain perspective and strength?

WHAT'S YOUR
DEFINITION OF
FULL-TIME MINISTRY?

COREY CLEEK

GENERAL MANAGEMENT, PASSALONG NETWORKS

55

*Just as each of us has one body with many members, and these members
do not all have the same function, so in Christ we who are many form
one body, and each member belongs to all the others.*

ROMANS 12:4-5

During the summer after I completed my MBA, as I was
devoting the majority of my time to starting a Christian ministry organization with a group of graduate school friends,
I took a step back to consider whether God was calling me
into full-time ministry or calling me into the marketplace
(interesting time to consider this, wasn't it?).

At the time, my limited definition of full-time ministry
included being on staff at a church or working full time for

a nonprofit Christian organization, and I was wrestling with the eternal value of spending the majority of my time working in the marketplace.

After some serious reflection, lots of prayer, and guidance from mentors, I realized that I was indeed being called to be in full-time ministry . . . in the marketplace!

This realization that I could be in full-time ministry in the marketplace altered my entire mind-set about business, ministry and my calling. For the first time, I had peace about spending the majority of my time in the business world, and I realized that reflecting God in my life can be expressed in various for-profit and nonprofit settings over time.

I've also learned that full-time ministry has more to do with serving God and others in the environment in which I've been placed than it does with my involvement in a particular vocation, organization or business.

How do you view your life as a business professional? Is it a job? A calling? A passion? A ministry?

During this time of reflection, I realized that for me, it is all of the above.

POINT TO PONDER

IT IS POSSIBLE FOR BUSINESS PROFESSIONALS TO
ALSO BE FULL-TIME MINISTERS.

QUESTIONS TO CONSIDER

193

1. Do you consider yourself to be in full-time ministry? How is your workplace a place of ministry for you right now?

2. How does Romans 12:4-8 validate or alter your perspective of why you are expressing your gifts in the way you are today?

3. If you have never considered yourself in full-time ministry, what could you do to change your perspective?

Panoramic View

MARKET INTELLIGENCE, CISCO SYSTEMS

56

From one man he made every nation of men, that they
should inhabit the whole earth; and he determined the times
set for them and the exact places where they should live.

ACTS 17:26

Although I am truly a people person, I have the tendency to become very task-oriented and efficiency-minded at work. When I am up against a deadline, I can live as though my highest calling is to make things happen in order to deliver quality on time.

I sometimes become so focused on the immediate that I forget the importance of people and relationships in my work environment. When I finally stop and take stock, I realize my eyes have once again shifted from seeking to be a part of my Father's vast and divinely perfect plans to my tunnel-vision attention to tasks and deadlines.

While a commitment to deadlines and a pride in my work are no doubt honoring to God, a purpose too narrowly defined for my work is not. I must constantly seek the Lord's help to remind me that I am part of a vastly bigger story that He is writing.

Although God's panoramic view of history, the present, the future and our unique role in the midst of it is something we cannot fully grasp this side of heaven, the Bible provides several encouraging words.

Acts 17:26 tells us that God has appointed the exact time when we are born and the place in which we live. Psalm 139:13,16 reminds us that He has constructed the very fiber of our being, knit us together and preordained our days. Ephesians 2:10 further encourages us that we are God's workmanship, created in Christ Jesus to do good works that God prepared in advance for us to do.

What powerful truths! We are each uniquely created in a way that is optimal, when coupled with God's grace, to do the works, touch the lives, spread the light, claim the territory and have the eternal Kingdom impact that God has desired for us since the beginning of time. When I meditate on these truths and remember that God has placed me in my workplace with divine intention, I am confronted by how critical it is to pray over my company!

195

My prayer is that God will place a burden on our hearts for people in our places of work and help us build relationships with those individuals whose lives He wants to touch through us. I also pray that He will give us divine appointments and open our eyes to His bigger plans.

POINT TO PONDER

GOD'S REASON FOR PLACING US IN OUR JOB AT
THIS TIME AND WITH THE PEOPLE AROUND US
HAS AN ETERNAL SIGNIFICANCE.

QUESTIONS TO CONSIDER

1. For what eternal good might God have placed you in your specific job at this time?

2. Why is it critical for you to pray over your company and invite God to work in it today?

3. A personal relationship with Jesus comes with influence on those around you. How does it feel to be part of the bigger plan of God?

TRUE IDENTITY

JIM BAKER
PRESIDENT, TELEION CAPITAL, LLC

57

But when the time had fully come, God sent his Son,
born of a woman, born under law, to redeem those under law,
that we might receive the full rights of sons.

GALATIANS 4:4-5

Over the years, I have come to realize how closely my identity is tied to the way I look at my business. As president and cofounder of an investment management firm, it is easy for me to fall into the trap of having my identity wrapped up in the degree of success of our firm.

Every day, I know how well our fund is doing. When my identity is wrapped up in my professional life, my success is linked to whether our investments' performance is up or down. Worry, fear and a lack of joy can easily creep into my life when I am not focused on my *true identity*. When this occurs, not only do *I* suffer, but my wife and children are also able to tell whether Dad had a "good/up" or "bad/down" day.

Fortunately, my true identity is as a son of God. In Galatians 4:6-7, Paul writes, "Because you are sons, God sent the Spirit of his Son into our hearts, the Spirit who calls out, 'Abba, Father.' So you are no longer a slave, but a son; and since you are a son, God has made you also an heir."

As Christians, we are sons and daughters and heirs of God. When I am focused on my true identity, my whole outlook on life is transformed. My temporal view with a focus on my life is changed to an eternal perspective with a focus on my Father's kingdom. My focus changes from living to please people to living to please God.

Another great byproduct of knowing and focusing on my true identity is having the peace that passes all understanding (see Philippians 4:7). It is much easier to deal with disappointments and uncertainty when I know that I am called to just do my best. I can leave the rest up to Him.

It is a constant challenge to keep my focus on God and my true identity. The key for me is starting my day with a quiet time. This time in prayer and reading the Bible sets the tone for my day. Without this quality time, I am quick to forget who I am in Christ and return to my self-absorbed life.

I pray that the Holy Spirit will empower us to spend time with our Father and to discover our true identity as a child of God.

POINT TO PONDER

OUR IDENTITY AS A CHILD OF GOD
WILL DRIVE OUR ATTITUDE ON LIFE.

QUESTIONS TO CONSIDER

199

1. What can you do to focus on your true identity as a son or daughter of God?

2. How do our self-absorbed identities impact our professional careers and our personal lives?

3. How does your true identity impact your professional career? How does it impact your personal life?

Do I Need to Know That Person?

Scott Malone

Underwriting Section Manager, State Farm Insurance

58

Whoever wants to become great among you must be your servant,
and whoever wants to be first must be slave of all.

Mark 10:43-44

My assignment was to give our new manager a quick tour
of my division. Being a new supervisor, I was a little nervous and wanted to make sure I made a good impression for
my sake and the sake of my area.

As we progressed on our tour, the lead worker from our
mail/forms area passed us, and we exchanged pleasant greet-
ings. After she continued on her way, the manager turned
to me and asked a question that stopped me in my tracks.
"Do I need to know that person?" she asked.

As soon as I heard it, I knew what she meant. She wanted to know whether that person was "worthy" of her time

and attention in order to help her move up the corporate ladder. "Yes," I replied, "she is probably the most important person in the entire division. If she were not here, the entire area would be negatively affected!"

When I told her that the person she just met was in our mail/forms area, she had a puzzled look on her face. It was as if she wanted to say, "Why would I be concerned with one of the lower-level employees?"

This encounter had a profound impact on me, and my philosophy for living out my faith at work. As a member of management, do I treat my coworkers with respect without regard to their status in the hierarchy? Do my daily inter-actions with all levels of employees demonstrate that I see them as equally important and needed? Am I willing to give of myself for their sake?

It is interesting to see that modern-day believers are not the only ones to struggle with status and position. On sever-al occasions we see the disciples, in the very presence of Jesus, jockeying for position. Just like many believers today, they fell into the trap of focusing on personal greatness rather than on serving God. Their priority seemed to be building themselves up rather than building up Christ by serving in His name.

Jesus' response seemed totally opposite from what the world and culture expected: To be a true leader, you must be a servant. The exciting part of the story is that Jesus not

201

only said it, but He also lived it!

Whether you are an entry-level employee or a CEO, your position in Christ is the same. How you treat others and view them can have a profound impact on whether others see Christ in you or view you as just another employee who is willing to step on them as you climb your way up in the company.

POINT TO PONDER

RESPECTFUL TREATMENT OF COWORKERS DEMONSTRATES OUR DESIRE TO SERVE GOD IN ALL REALMS OF LIFE, INCLUDING OUR WORK.

QUESTIONS TO CONSIDER

1. Does your view and treatment of others at work demonstrate your respect for them despite their position?

2. How is the corporate ladder of success different from God's ladder of success?

3. Romans 12:10 says, "Honor one another above yourselves." How does this verse speak to equality among workers?

A Christian Example in the Workplace

Larry Allhands

DIRECTOR, CUSTOMER ENGINEERING, APPRION, INC.

59

*Be careful, however, that the exercise of your freedom does
not become a stumbling block to the weak.*

1 CORINTHIANS 8:9

"I'm sorry," I said to my coworker. "On ethical grounds, I just can't do that." He had just asked me if I could install a program on his computer for which he had no license. I valued his friendship so much that I could not comply with his request. It was difficult for me, but it was an act of love.

Throughout each day, we are confronted with hundreds of decisions. Depending on our profession or vocation, the decisions we face range from as small as whether or not to hit the snooze button in the morning to whether or not to close a plant and impact thousands of people's jobs. Each decision we make ultimately shapes the outcome of our day.

But as Christians, it is not only our day we are affecting. Ultimately, it is the shape of eternity itself that hangs in the balance in even the smallest decision.

In business environments, there are certain values, standards and behavior patterns deemed "normal" by the world. In order to prosper in these environments, it is necessary for us to adopt many of these standards. Of course, this can be problematic because we are held under intense scrutiny by the seekers, new believers and unbelievers around us.

Everyone has an intrinsic knowledge of how someone who professes to be a follower of Christ should act. We are viewed and judged by those standards. Although some may not know the Scriptures, they expect to see something in our lives that is missing in theirs.

Nearly 2,000 years ago, Paul dealt directly with this very same issue in 1 Corinthians 8:9-13. He stated that he was fully aware that others watched, judged and imitated his daily behavior. The topic of the passage may have been about eating meat offered to idols, but the subject was about setting a godly example by not partaking in behavior that would become a stumbling block for the weak or cause another to fall into sin.

Paul correctly concluded that regardless of the legality of eating the meat under God's law, the real argument was that the effect of one's actions on another person's walk takes precedence. He further stated that he would never take part in behavior that might give the appearance of sin if it would harm another.

So, armed with this understanding, we ought to be more circumspect in our daily decision-making process. God's love on Earth manifests itself through our behavior. It is a true act of love to be conscious of and submit to another's need.

POINT TO PONDER

WE MAY BE THE ONLY CHRISTIAN EXAMPLE
SOMEONE IS EXPOSED TO DURING THEIR DAY.

QUESTIONS TO CONSIDER

1. What activities do you currently participate in that could cause a brother or sister to stumble?

2. If God's love on Earth manifests itself through our actions, how does that understanding change your perspective of everything you do?

3. How should this perspective inform your habits and relationships with your coworkers and clients?

PROCESS VERSUS PARTICULARS

EXECUTIVE VICE PRESIDENT, TORQUIN, LLC

60

Testing will refine, cleanse, and purify those who keep their heads
on straight and stay true, for there is still more to come.
DANIEL 11:35, *THE MESSAGE*

As a serial entrepreneur, I have started and built a number of companies and business concepts. It is exciting to see a vision of what could be actually come into being. Quite often, however, I'm stunned and amazed by the many difficulties and challenges I encounter in pursuit of these dreams.

What I have come to appreciate is that these problems are almost always opportunities for me to cooperate with God as He actively refines things in my life. As He did with His own Son, the Father actually allows us to be tested in order to build our most fundamental muscles: our character and our faith. He also tests us so that by our example we might be an encouragement to others who will face similar issues down the road.

Over time, I've learned to step back and ask God, "What are You teaching me at this point in life?" I once accepted a job in Texas that I thought to be ideal. After only two weeks, I found it to be the worst job I ever had. So I asked God what He was teaching me or what process He was taking me through. His response was, "I'm using this current job to break you of your addiction to work."

He was right. I had become addicted to the rush and thrill of the workplace. I had enjoyed it more than being a good husband, father and friend. So I said, "Alright, Lord, I've learned this lesson." But He knew differently. Five months later, when I had truly been broken, He finally allowed me to leave that position and get a job in which I thrived for many years after.

Becoming more aware of the overall process of being refined and purified provides us with a powerful perspective on our current situation. It also allows us to rise above the noise level of the particulars of the day. Those of us who keep our cool and stay true in the midst of extreme difficulties will influence many around us through our example.

Asking God for His extended view—for Him to reveal His plans and purposes for our lives—will give us the hope and courage we need to continue pressing into the challenges at hand. It will keep us humble, knowing that we will be sustained by His grace alone. Win or lose, succeed or fail—these are not the economics of the kingdom of God. His measure of success is a humble and obedient spirit that hears His voice and responds to it.

God's eye is searching the earth right now for such a right-minded, responsive and willing heart (see Psalm 53:2). Why not offer Him yours again right now?

POINT TO PONDER

ONLY THROUGH GOD'S EXTENDED VIEW CAN WE SEE HIS
PLANS AND PURPOSES FOR OUR LIFE.

QUESTIONS TO CONSIDER

1. What is God currently refining out of your life or pouring into your life?

2. What obstacles are you currently facing that could be seen as opportunities for change and growth?

3. How can you step back today and take a different view of your life and your work?

CONTRIBUTORS

Larry Allhands is the director of customer engineering for Apprion, Inc., an industrial wireless automation company, and serves in the California Army National Guard as a Nuclear/Biological/Chemical Warfare Specialist. He enjoys working with teenagers and shares a passion with his wife, Gina, for serving the Lord in his community.

Cheryl Bachelder retired three years ago from her position as president of KFC restaurants. She presently serves as a consultant to the Women's Foodservice Forum, and she has a very full life raising three daughters aged 12, 14 and 20.

Jim Baker is president of Teleion Capital, LLC, an investment management firm. Jim and his wife have three children and reside in Nashville, Tennessee. He enjoys coaching and playing sports and serves as an elder in his church.

Todd Barr is blessed to have two young sons, Wilson and Owen, and a fantastic wife, Jessica. He is director of enterprise marketing at Red Hat, a leading provider of Linux® and open source technology.

Brian Bates is an assignment manager for WTVF-TV, the CBS affiliate in Nashville, Tennessee. Since he first started at the station in 1995, he has held a variety of jobs within the company, including associate producer, producer and his current position as assignment manager.

Wes Bolsen is a senior associate with McKinsey and Company, a management consulting firm with more than 86 locations in 46 countries around the world. He loves the outdoors and great dinners with friends.

Alex Brubaker is the managing director of Brubaker Consulting. His career includes stints as a strategy consultant, biotech entrepreneur, writer, high-tech marketer and independent consultant. He holds an MBA from Stanford and undergraduate degrees in Finance and Mechanical Engineering from the University of Pennsylvania. He lives in San Jose, California, and is passionate about his family and soccer.

Regi Campbell resides in Atlanta, Georgia, where he is an elder at North Point Community Church. As a principal at Seedsower Investments, he invests in technology-enabled start-up companies. Regi is also author of *About My Father's Business—Taking Your Faith to Work*.

Rachel Carriere is a native of Atlanta, Georgia, and currently resides in Seattle, Washington. After receiving her MBA,

Rachel spent several years with Amazon.com before becoming a senior associate at Point B Solutions Group, LLP, a consulting firm that specializes in project leadership and execution. Outside of work, Rachel enjoys the outdoors, running and playing her violin.

Corey Cleek has held various U.S. and international marketing and business development positions at eBay and amazon.com. He is presently a general manager for a digital media start-up as a part of PassAlong Networks in Nashville, Tennessee, and is an active angel investor in Internet media and e-commerce companies. Corey's primary passions are exploring the intersection of faith and business, developing new businesses and non-profit ministry organizations, attending major sporting events, and playing soccer.

Cindy Comperry, a native Tennessean, currently resides in Nashville. After spending many years in fundraising for the American Cancer Society, she is currently an advertising sales project manager for Journal Communications.

Shelly Culpepper's passion is learning to raise a spiritually strong family. Before becoming a mom, she raised funds for the Cleveland Clinic Taussig Cancer Center, received her MBA from Duke University, and later worked in marketing for General Motors, and for LifeScan, Inc., a Johnson and Johnson Company. She and her husband, Spence, and two children, Kendall and T.J., live in Walnut Creek, California.

Gary Daichendt, former executive vice president of Cisco Systems, has a passion to see successful Christian business executives in the marketplace. Gary has over 25 years of experience in the high-tech industry and currently serves on the boards of several companies.

Ed Diffendal is a director of business development at Symantec Software. Since early adulthood, he has enjoyed rock climbing and mountaineering. Ed has reached the highest summit on every continent and climbed El Cap four times. Ed prefers light and fast mountain solos, where no one is forced to smell his feet.

Dianne Eckloff asked Christ into her heart in June 2004 and left her position as senior director of Experian shortly thereafter to pursue a personal business. She is the founder and president of Boswell Basset, Inc., and also devotes her time to the Silicon Valley-based equip organization, which helps business leaders integrate their faith and careers.

Al Erisman is director of the Center for Integrity in Business at Seattle Pacific University and cofounder and editor of *Ethix* (www.ethix.org). Prior to his current role, Al spent 32 years at The Boeing Company, the last 10 as director of research and development for mathematics and computing technology. Al and his wife, Nancy, have been married for 44 years and have 4 children and 7 grandchildren.

Keith Ferrin is the founder and president of True Success Coaching, LLC. He teaches workshops, speaks at conferences and coaches individuals and corporations in the area of public communication. Keith and his family live outside of Seattle, Washington.

Allison Flexer is currently the director of financial and operational analysis at MedTel International, a healthcare company based in Franklin, Tennessee. Allison has been a Certified Public Accountant since 1999 and holds a BBA in accounting from Belmont University in Nashville, Tennessee.

David Friedman spent the last several years advising governments and Global 1000 companies on foreign direct investment strategies as a managing director in the consulting group at CB Richard Ellis. Prior to moving to Manhattan, David was a technology entrepreneur in Silicon Valley. Today, David is a senior consultant at Oxford Analytica and lives with his wife, Maxine, in Manhattan.

Amy Fritz is a principal at Strategic Dialogues, a business consulting and market research company. Amy is a native Californian, born and raised in the San Francisco Bay area, and has an MBA from Santa Clara University. Amy enjoys teaching and coaching entrepreneurs.

Craig Fryar is the executive vice president of Torquin, LLC, a drug discovery and IP development company headquartered in Austin, Texas. Prior to joining Torquin, Craig was involved in Austin's venture capital community, assisting entrepreneurs in creating strategies, tactics and teams to attract venture capital funding. He has over 20 years of business development and "technology evangelism" experience.

Pat Gelsinger is a senior vice president and general manager of the Digital Enterprise Group of the Intel Corporation. Pat has worked at Intel for the past 27 years and works in both an executive and a technical role. He is also active in the Christian community and is the author of *Balancing Your Faith, Family and Work*.

Rodney Gibson IV is a director at Archstone-Smith, a multifamily real estate investment trust based in Denver, Colorado. Rodney recently finished his MBA at Wharton College and is currently helping in Archstone-Smith's management development program.

Erick Goss is vice president of marketing for Magazines.com, an e-commerce company that specializes in selling magazine subscriptions via the Internet. Prior to Magazines.com, Erick worked for Amazon.com and for the U.S. Navy. He resides in Nashville, Tennessee, with his wife, Lisa, and two daughters, and attends Grace Community Church.

Tom Horvath is chairman of Berkeley Court Advisers, a business consulting firm that works with organizations to integrate three business fundamentals—Strategy, Talent and Execution. Through consulting and teaching, Tom lives out his life-purpose of inspiring excellence in others. He lives in Orlando, Florida, with his wife and his two sons.

Brett Johnson is the president of The Institute for Innovation, Integration and Impact, a strategic consulting firm. He and his wife also founded equip, a ministry that mobilizes and equips businesspeople to use their skills in business-as-missions. Brett is the author of *Convergence* and *LEMON Leadership* and the coauthor of *I-Operations*.

Manka Johnson is a partner at OneAccord, a management consulting firm headquartered near Seattle, Washington, where she works with technology companies to discover and capture new market opportunities to drive revenue growth. She lives in San Francisco, California.

Danny Kapic is an investment sales broker at Marcus & Millichap Real Estate Investment Brokerage Company, where he specializes in investment sales of properties. He and his wife, Emily, live in Sacramento, California, and enjoy exploring the world through adventure travels together.

Gabe Knapp grew up on a farm near Ord, Nebraska, and is currently senior product manager in the Windows Marketing Division at Microsoft Corporation. He holds a Bachelor of Science degree from Trinity University in San Antonio, Texas, and an MBA from Harvard Business School.

216

Nancy Lai is an MBA candidate at the Wharton School and an MA candidate at the Lauder Institute at the University of Pennsylvania. After graduation, Nancy hopes to pursue a career in business in China. She enjoys community, photography and the outdoors.

Barry Landis is president of the Landis Agency, an entertainment consulting firm based in Nashville, Tennessee, where he lives with his wife, Sarah, and two boys, Sean and Justin. Barry has worked with Warner Brothers and Word Records for 20 years and has recently consulted with Sony/BMG, Provident/Integrity and Vanderbilt University.

Gary Layne is president of The Perfect Clone, Inc., and the founder of Out Loud Ministries. Gary is passionate about

Christians living out their faith and travels the country challenging Christians to live out loud for Jesus Christ. He resides in Marietta, Georgia, with his wife, Carol, and kids.

Billy Leonard is a production manager and TV show host at Overseas Radio and Television. He and his wife, Yen Ling, live in Taipei, Taiwan, with their two daughters, Annabelle and Savannah.

Andy Liu formerly ran NetConversions, a provider of website usability technology and services, until the company was acquired by aQuantive, Inc., in 2003. Andy is currently the CEO of Advanced Media Research Group, Inc., and the chairman of Future Hope, a nonprofit organization. He attends Quest Church in Seattle, Washington, and is a huge fan of Seattle sports.

Scott Malone is an underwriting section manager for State Farm Insurance and also serves as director of implementation and training at His Church at Work, a ministry that works with churches to help establish and grow WorkLife Ministries. He and his family reside in Cumming, Georgia.

Ryan MacCarthy is a high-tech entrepreneur who lives in the Silicon Valley area. He spends his days leading products and community for AnchorFree, a company that provides consumers and businesses with the nation's largest network of free wi-fi access to the Internet, and his weekends building companies with Nebo Group. He is passionate about his wife, free wi-fi, snowboarding and building businesses that impact the Kingdom.

Mark McClain is the founder and CEO of SailPoint Technologies, an enterprise software company that specializes in security and identity management. Mark was the founder and president of Waveset Technologies, and after its acquisition by Sun Microsystems, served as senior vice president of marketing at Sun.

Katie McNerney is a marketing manager at eBay, where she manages an e-commerce consulting program for small businesses. She has a passion for economic development in the developing world and recently returned from a volunteer consulting trip to Jakarta, Indonesia, with equip. Katie is originally from Virginia and currently lives in San Francisco, California.

Jedd Medefind lives with his wife, Rachel, and two daughters, Siena and Marin, in Washington, DC. He has worked internationally and domestically in American government and politics and is currently the director of a national initiative in the U.S. Government. Jedd is the author of several books, including *Four Souls* and *The Revolutionary Communicator*.

Brent Milligan is a Nashville-based record producer and session player. He has worked on many gold and platinum albums and plays tennis whenever possible. He married his high school sweetheart and has three children.

Duane Moyer is the executive vice president of His Church at Work. A native of Silicon Valley, Duane is passionate about experiencing God in his work life and loves mountain biking, hiking and being with people. He married his high school sweetheart at age 22 and has 3 awesome children.

Molly Nonnenberg is a human resources manager at Applied Biosystems, located in the San Francisco Bay Area. She enjoys being involved in ministry to high school students at Peninsula Bible Church in Cupertino, California.

Carolyn Norton is program coordinator for the Coca-Cola Scholars Foundation in Atlanta, Georgia, an affiliate of the Coca-Cola Company that provides college scholarships to students. Her hobbies include photography, poetry, scrapbooking, traveling (especially on mission trips) and being a fun aunt to her five nieces and nephews in Richmond, Virginia.

Monica Patrick is a procurement analyst for the ConocoPhillips Company. She has worked in oil and gas since 1998, focusing her attention on procurement. She was recently married, and she and her husband are actively involved in their local church, serving primarily in children's ministry. She has also been an active participant in Priority Associates, a ministry of Campus Crusade for Christ that challenges and equips Christian professionals in the marketplace to be Kingdom minded.

Randy Raggio is assistant professor of marketing at the E. J. Ourso College of Business, Louisiana State University, in Baton Rouge, Lousiana. He was previously the marketing director for Kidpower, the company that produced the Funnoodle (those long, brightly colored foam pool noodles). During the summer of 1999, Randy spent seven weeks helping to set up daycare centers in the slums of Bombay, India, and was actively involved in managing the project for several years.

Reagan Rylander is a project manager in real estate and community development. He lives in Austin, Texas, where he pursues God at the intersection of real estate, music, entrepreneurship and ministry.

Kevon Saber is a passionate entrepreneur and a founding executive of GenPlay Games. His interests include Kingdom unity, holistic discipleship, tennis and ballroom dancing.

Doug Schweitzer is a graduate of Tennessee Temple University and is currently the President and CEO of Arthur Douglas

Apparel, Inc., a fine men's clothing firm. Doug is passionate about using his life to disciple and mentor young men into becoming mature men of God. His favorite hobbies include outdoor sports, but he enjoys nothing more than spending time with his wife, Lori, and their two children, Ryan and Jenna.

Gene Shackelford is a former plant manager at Union Carbide. After a 36-year career in the petrochemical industry, Gene moved to Austin, Texas, and became involved with Campus Crusade for Christ. This led to a rewarding four-year experience for Gene and his wife, Frances, as they served in ministry in Mozambique, Africa.

Brian Shepler serves as chief financial officer for Ronald Blue & Company, a leading provider of wealth management services with a distinct emphasis on biblical stewardship. Brian is a director of Lighthouse Family Retreat and Halftime of Georgia. He and his wife, Cindy, live in Atlanta, Georgia, and are enjoying parenting two young children.

Tom Tison graduated from Liberty University with a Bachelor of Science degree in accounting, then became a sales manager with Thomas Nelson Publisher's Varsity Internship Program. Currently, he runs Tison and Shelton Consulting, a benefits and insurance consulting firm. Tom lives with his wife, Christy, and his three young sons in Knoxville, Tennessee.

Ray Tong is a certified public accountant with an MBA in finance from Duke University. Recently, Ray began running triathlons, and he enjoys teaching adult Sunday School. He is a husband and a father of three boys.

Melissa Utter works in market intelligence at Cisco Systems. She is originally from the San Francisco Bay area and has worked as a market analyst at technology-oriented companies for the past seven years. Melissa enjoys the great outdoors, travel and foreign languages. She also has a deep longing to help others discover their potential.

Virendra Vase is in general management at Experian and has been involved with high-tech software companies for over 15 years. His areas of passion include marriage, family, business as ministry/missions, micro-enterprise, evangelism and small groups. Virendra has been married to his wife, Kim, for 14 years and has three children.

Jon Venverloh resides in the San Francisco Bay area with his wife and children. His career has included stints at worldwide advertising agencies, Internet startups and Google, where he currently structures strategic partnerships. Jon serves on the board of directors of the Vineyard Christian Church, plays bass guitar in its band, and loves snow skiing, mountain biking and playing squash.

Elisabeth Wadsworth enjoys encouraging others to use their professional gifting for spiritual goals. After working in banking on the East Coast, Elisabeth moved to California to pursue her passion: developing infrastructure in inner cities. Elisabeth is currently working as a consultant to the healthcare industry as she pursues her MBA in Philadelphia.

Chris Widener is the president and CEO of Made for Success. He is the author of eight books on leadership and motivation and is co-host, along with Zig Ziglar, of the TV show *True Performance*.

Allen Wolf is an award-winning filmmaker and board-game creator. He is the founder and president of Morning Star Pictures and Morning Star Games.

Bruce Woolsey is vice president of Avenue A/Razorfish, a digital marketing services and technology firm. He has worked in interactive marketing for the past eight years and currently resides in Seattle, Washington. He is the very proud—and very exhausted—father of three boys.

Michael Yang is a high-tech entrepreneur and the founder and president of Become.com, a shopping search-engine. Michael lives with his wife, Sunny, and their son, David, in Los Altos Hills, California.

Become a Devotional Ventures contributor.

Provide comments and feedback.

Connect with marketplace ministries—
local, national and international.

The journey continues at
www.devotionalventures.org